SEDGEFORD AERODROME AND THE AERIAL CONFLICT OVER NORTH WEST NORFOLK
IN THE FIRST WORLD WAR

FOR ROHAN

SEDGEFORD AERODROME
and the aerial conflict over North West Norfolk during the First World War

Gary Rossin

*Further details of Poppyland Publishing titles can be found at
www.poppyland.co.uk
where clicking on the 'Support and Resources' button will lead to pages
specially compiled to support this title.*

POPPYLAND
PUBLISHING

ISBN 978 1 90979642 3
Published by Poppyland Publishing, Lowestoft, NR32 3BB

Picture credits:

Unless otherwise indicated, all pictures are from the SHARP archive or collection.

Gary Rossin: All maps and diagrams, Plates 1.6, 1.7, 1.9, 1.10, 2.1, 2.2, 2.3, 2.2, 2.4, 2.5, 2.8, 2.9, 2.10, 2.14, 2.15, 2.16, 2.17, 3.9, 4.11, 4.12, 4.13, 4.14, 6.1, 6.2, 6.5, 6.6, 6.7, 6.8, 6.9, 6.10, 6.11, 6.12, 6.13, 6.14, 6.15, 6.16, 6.17, 6.18, 6.20, 6.21, 6.22, 6.23, 6.24, 6.25. 6.26, 6.27, 7.3, 7.4, 7.5, 7.6, 7.7, 7.8, 7.9, 7.10, 7.11, 7.12, 7.13, 7.14, 7.15, 7.16,
Rober Malster collection: Plate 3.8

Printed in the United Kingdom by Lightning Source.

Acknowledgements

The path to seeing this book published has been a long one and I would firstly like to thank everyone who has supported me in this undertaking. You all know who you are.

Specifically, I wish to thank Dr Neil Faulkner for his guidance, critical analysis and support throughout. Brian Fraser has been heavily involved with the recent research at Sedgeford aerodrome, reading initial drafts and for his knowledge of recording standing buildings which have been invaluable in producing this book and to my own education within the subject area.

The initial years of research on the Sedgeford aerodrome site was undertaken by several members of the Sedgeford Historical & Archaeological Research Project, all deserve thanks for commencing the path of discovery. The book draws from this team's knowledge and endeavours but any resulting mistakes contained are my own.

The Sedgeford Historical & Archaeological Research Project began in 1996 with the aim of researching the broad range of human settlement activity within what is a typical Norfolk parish. Since its humble beginnings, thousands of people have worked with the project. For many, such as myself, it offered them a first opportunity to 'do' archaeology. I will be forever grateful for the Project opening the door to me and I hope the door remains open to many more in future years.

During my research for this book I received valuable assistance from the Royal Air Force Museum at Hendon and the True's Yard Fisherfolk Museum.

Peter Stibbons, formerly at Poppyland Publishing has been immensely supportive and creative in turning raw words into the book you are reading now.

Finally, I must pay thanks to the landowner of the site, Mr. William Barber. Without his support and keen interest into the historical and archaeological background to the site, it would not have been possible to tell this story.

Gary Rossin
June 2018

Please note that the Sedgeford Aerodrome site is on private land and access is not open to the general public.

Contents

Foreword

The news is filled with images of war. As often as not, they involve airpower, mass destruction, bodies in the rubble, and streams of ragged refugees. We have grown used to aerial bombing and the targeting of civilians as intrinsic to warfare.

But this kind of industrialised killing is barely a century old. And when it started, the technology was so primitive, the bombs so few, so lightweight, so crudely dropped, that casualties were mercifully few. Yet the shock was visceral: the dropping of aerial bombs on towns and villages where ordinary folk lived evoked tabloid headlines about 'baby killers' and threats of vengeance against 'the Hun'. And where was this? Where did a century of aerial bombing of civilian settlements begin?

In East Anglia, on the night of 19 January 1915, when Zeppelin L-3 bombed Great Yarmouth, and her sister airship, Zeppelin L-4, bombed its way along the north Norfolk coast as far as King's Lynn.

This book, by my friend and colleague Gary Rossin, who has been Project Director of the Sedgeford Historical and Archaeological Research Project (SHARP) for ten years, is about the history and archaeology of the air war over north-west Norfolk between 1915 and 1918. It is about the origins of a new way of war – one that no longer restricted death and destruction to defined battlefields contested by soldiers, but spread it so widely, using modern technologies of killing, that entire societies might be consumed by it.

For sure, what happened in north-west Norfolk during the Great War was as nothing compared with what was to come – in the Blitz, in the carpet bombing of Germany, in the firebombing of Tokyo, in the atomic destruction of Hiroshima and Nagasaki, in the saturation bombing of Vietnam and Cambodia. But it pointed the way, and, imprinted in the archaeological remains all around us this little corner of East Anglia, we can see the baby steps of 20th century airpower.

North-west Norfolk was not only one of the targets of history's first strategic bombing raid; it was also in the forefront of pioneering efforts to forge the first home-defence system, complete with a wireless-listening early warning system and squadrons of night fighters stationed at local aerodromes.

Thanks to the willing support of local farmer William Barber, SHARP archaeologists have been investigating the remains of Sedgeford Aerodrome over many years. The results of this work, combined with the evidence of maps, photos, and contemporary records, provide the core of this book.

But Gary has done more than simply tell the story of one aerodrome. He has placed it in the wider context of the air war over north-west Norfolk, beginning with a detailed account of the terror attack on the night of 19 January 1915, then reporting on the development of the early warning system, centred on the Hunstanton cliffs, before charting the dynamic history of the aerodrome itself, which began life as a night landing-ground, ended the First World War as a major training facility with more than a thousand service personnel in residence, and then resumed its military life a generation later as a decoy airfield during the Second World War.

This excellent volume syntheses several years of historical and archaeological research which have highlighted north-west Norfolk's role in the development of modern industrialised warfare. Undoubtedly, the story it has to tell is of great local interest; but it is a story with global implications.

Dr. Neil Faulkner FSA

Founding-Director, Sedgeford Historical and Archaeological Research Project

Introduction

Shortly before 8.00pm on the cold winter's night of 19th January, 1915, the prevailing silence along the north Norfolk coastline was broken by the unfamiliar, deep drone of diesel engines passing high overhead. Within the hour, another alien, albeit more terrifying, noise would be heard in towns and villages in east and west Norfolk. This would be the sound of bombs exploding; destroying buildings, injuring and killing their inhabitants. This quiet area of Norfolk had become victim to the first German Zeppelin airship raid on mainland Britain.

The First World War redrew the rules of war. This was to be the first conflict in military history that would be fought under the edict of 'total war'. A war which would bring an aerial campaign to innocent civilians; a war of terror, where the impending threat caused nearly as much trauma as the actual casualties. A war which brought the conflict's frontline to Norfolk and other areas of Britain.

The threat, often hidden by the night sky, of the Zeppelin was not the only new arrival to be seen in the wartime skies above west Norfolk. Barely ten years prior to the start of the First World War, two American brothers, Orville and Wilbur Wright, had successfully achieved the first successful heavier-than-air powered flight in an aircraft, the *Flyer I*. Yet at the outbreak of the war, aircraft which had already evolved dramatically from the Wright Brothers' initial design were being given their first of many military roles. Just like they would be during the Second World War, the skies of Norfolk would soon be full of strange looking aircraft; set on attempting to defend against the German Zeppelin menace or training fledgling pilots to fight in foreign skies where the conflict would rage for four more years.

This book is in two sections. The first examines the events of the main Zeppelin raids on the Norfolk coastline, studying the German airships used to undertake these raids of terror and investigating the impact of these attacks on the local communities. This section also investigates how the British Home Defence force tried to repel the aerial threat. It also studies how yet another embryonic technology during the First World War, wireless telegraphy, was applied by the British along the clifftops at Hunstanton.

The second part of the book closely investigates the archaeological research that has been undertaken at Sedgeford aerodrome. Starting life as a modest airfield created to defend against the German Zeppelin threat, it rapidly expanded into a large training aerodrome of over 1,200 personnel, teaching new generations of pilots military combat skills before they transferred to war's front line. The airfield's later more clandestine role which it carried out during the Second World War is also examined.

Professor Nicholas J. Saunders, Professor of Material Culture at Bristol University, describes Modern Conflict Archaeology as 'the involving the interdisciplinary study of conflict and its legacies during the 20th and early 21st centuries, not restricted to battlefields, or to large-scale wars between nations, but embracing every kind of conflict and its diversity of social and cultural legacies'. The latter part of this book is devoted to the archaeological study of the site. Although many British WWI airfields have been examined historically, few offer the opportunity to study the archaeological record of the site. This book investigates how the site grew from a modest field with a motley collection of timber buildings into a three-squadron aerodrome covering almost 120 acres and home to over 1,200 personnel.

For over eight years a small team from the Sedgeford Historical & Archaeological Research Project (SHARP) has been working on the aerodrome site, recording the many (and at times ephemeral) features that remain there. This study investigates the daily lives of the men who served (and died there), the aircraft they flew and the archaeological 'footprints' they left behind. The documentary archive for Sedgeford's WWI and WWI role is not expansive; as such the recording process of certain buildings has not always been a straightforward one. Aligned to this, many of the original buildings were either completely removed or stripped down to their foundations following the Armistice.

Recording and surveying of the site continues to this day. Each excavation brings new discoveries and new interpretations which add to our understanding of the site. Details of current activity being under taken by SHARP can be found at www.sharp.org.uk.

Fig. 0.1. A map of Norfolk locating the Sedgeford site.

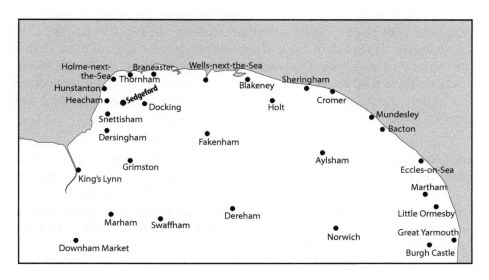

Chapter 1

The Zeppelin L-3 Raid

Soon after noon on Tuesday 19th January, 1915 three large, dark shapes appeared in the grey skies over the Dutch island of Ameland. The throbbing engine noises were from a still relatively new type of craft to be seen in the skies; the Zeppelin. As the airships moved westward over the icy North Sea towards the East Coast of Britain, those on the ground who had come out of their homes to observe these strange craft were watching history in the making; the airships passing overhead were about to undertake the first aerial bombardment of the British Isles. A raid which would change the shape of warfare forever.

Christmas had come and gone and the war that everyone believed would have been over by then was showing no signs of concluding; quite the opposite in fact. This was a war that would be fought differently to all others; its scale, its tactics, its loss of life and its weaponry. Foremost amongst these changes was the aerial war. Barely twelve years before this cold January day, the Wright brothers had managed to achieve controlled and sustained flight (for 120 feet and of 12 seconds duration) and yet aerial warfare was now adding itself to the traditional methods combat previously carried out on land and sea.

In fairness, the airship had been around for a few years prior to the first successful flight of an aircraft. It had been a German aristocrat, Count Ferdinand von Zeppelin, who had invented and developed the rigid airship that would become associated with his name. His first airship, the LZ-1 had flown in July 1900 but Zeppelin had struggled to convince the German armed forces that the airship could play a key role within the climate of military development that was sweeping the country. At the outbreak of WWI, the German Army began using airships in reconnaissance roles over land but quickly saw the

Plate 1.1
Count Ferdinand Adolf Heinrich August Graf von Zeppelin, German general and inventor, who founded the Zeppelin airship company and whose name was to become synonymous with airship design.

damage that could be inflicted by ground fire. This adverse experience saw them quickly withdraw the airships from an operational role. However, at roughly the same time, the German Navy were exploring the benefits of the airship as a scouting cruiser, in preparation of the expected British naval blockade of its North Sea ports. The German Navy quickly saw the potential for a new role for the Zeppelin and began to take on a greater responsibility in the airship's design and development.

Once hostilities had commenced, the German Army and Navy continued down their separate paths in airship development and strategy until their respective roles became defined. The Army would concentrate on night attacks on enemy bases and railway junctions, along with the British ports that were supplying them. The Navy would focus on defensive reconnaissance. There was however a common cause that united officers of both services; and that was to extend the Zeppelin's role in order to bomb the enemy's cities and capitals.

On the 20th August, 1914, the Deputy Chief of German Naval Staff, Konteradmiral Paul Behncke visited Imperial Headquarters to seek permission to attack London. The German military's thinking was that such raids, then unknown in contemporary warfare, would cause absolute panic and hysteria amongst the population, thus bringing pressure to bear on the British government to end the war. A list of secondary targets had also been drawn up which included: Dover, Portsmouth, Humberside, Tyneside, Plymouth, Glasgow and the Firth of Forth. The desire to be the first service to attack mainland Britain developed into an intense rivalry between the German Army and Navy.

Plate 1.2
Kaiser Wilhelm II, German emperor and king of Prussia from 1888 to the end of World War I, who was to find himself leading his country to war against two of his first cousins, George V of Great Britain and Tsar Nicholas II of Russia.

Despite the entreaties of the German military, there remained a substantial obstacle for any attack on British soil; this was in the shape of the Kaiser Wilhelm II. Wilhelm II who was the grandson of Queen Victoria, found himself at the outbreak of war in August, 1914 leading his country into combat against two of his first cousins, George V of Great Britain and Tsar Nicholas II of Russia. In the eyes of the Kaiser, to be at war with his cousin's country was one thing but to be potentially dropping bombs on members of his own family was quite another. Other members of the German government were also supportive of the Kaiser's stance but more from the perspective that the thought of killing innocent woman and children through aerial bombardment was morally repugnant and totally unacceptable. This subject had already been debated at the Hague Conference of 1899, where a vote was passed prohibiting aircraft from discharging projectiles and explosives.

The contemporary mood of the German public had also been pulled towards the expanding of the role of what they perceived to be their mighty weapon. During the first months of the war, a rhyme became popular with German children:

> Zeppelin flieg,
> Hilf uns im Krieg,
> Fliege nach England,
> England wird abgebrannt,
> Zeppelin flieg!

> Fly Zeppelin,
> Fly to England,
> England shall be destroyed with fire!

However much the Kaiser rejected the plans for Zeppelin attacks on British cities, the voices within the German military did not abate and finally on 7th January, 1915 the pressure on the Kaiser to relax his view on raids succeeded. In giving his consent for raids to proceed there were to be strict conditions. Targets were only to include military sites or docks in the Lower Thames estuary or along the English coast. The Kaiser was extremely concerned and sensitive for the safety of his cousins in London, along with their royal palaces and the city's many historic monuments.

As soon as this green light had been received from German High Command, planning began for the attack on British soil. Within a week, the German Navy had formulated a plan that would see four Zeppelins launch an attack.

Plate 1.3
Zeppelin L-3 being returned to its shed at its base at Fuhlsbüttel

The raid was planned for Wednesday 13th January, 1915 but bad weather was to cause this to be postponed. A revised plan was quickly formulated to take place the following Tuesday; this time three airships would attack - Zeppelins L-3, L-4 and L-6. All three Zeppelins had been part of the previous week's postponed raid and although the weather forecast for the 19th January showed uncertain conditions, the order to proceed was given.

Zeppelin L-3 (factory designation LZ-24) was the third airship to be built by the German Navy and its only one in service when the war began; the previous two Zeppelins L-1 and L-2 having crashed at the end of 1913. L-3 had also been the first Zeppelin to undertake a specific wartime mission, conducting a reconnaissance flight off the Dutch coast on 11th August, 1914. A week later it had flown a further reconnaissance mission north as far as Ryvingen in Norway. Zeppelin L-3 measured 157m in length and had a maximum speed of 47.4 mph and carrying a crew of 14 it had a range of 1,366 miles. Zeppelin L-4 (factory designation LZ-27) was of similar dimensions and performance to that of L-3 and had made her maiden flight on the 28th August, 1914. The third of the Zeppelins to make up the raiding party was Zeppelin L-6 (factory designation LZ-31) and it had made its maiden flight on the 3rd November, 1914. All three airships had been built at Friedrichshafen and would be carrying enough fuel for a thirty hour return flight, along with individual payloads consisting of eight 110lb. high explosive bombs and 25 incendiaries each.

Plate 1.4
Zeppelin gunners keeping watch for enemy aircraft. In addition to carrying a deadly payload of bombs, the airship carried a formidable array of defensive machine guns.

A typical Zeppelin crew at this time consisted of between 16 and 25 members, depending on the size of the airship and its mission. All crew members would be either officers or NCOs and all would have volunteered to be part of a Zeppelin crew. Each member would have trained for six months, being assessed both individually and as a team, a key element of the assessment tests being an individual's medical suitability for altitude flying.

A typical Zeppelin crew comprised:

Commander – overall responsibility for the airship, targeting, bomb type selection and bomb release.

Executive Officer – navigation of the airship in and out of the hangar, communicating orders to the crew, watch duties.

Chief Engineer – management of airship mechanics, steersman, machine gun operator and sailmaker.

Observation Officer – management of wireless, telegraph and bombing equipment.

Wireless Operators – sending and receiving of orders, operating machine guns when required.

Steersman – operation of rudder and elevators, release of ballast, operating hydrogen valves, operating machine guns when required.

Sailmaker – maintenance and repair of gas cells and outer cover, release of gas valves.

Mechanics - operating engines, replenishment of engine fuel, oils and coolants, in flight maintenance and repairs.

In their aircrafts' hangars, the ground crew made their final checks on the airships, while outside the January weather showed no signs of improving. With cold, grey skies sweeping in from the west, this first aerial attack on British soil was certainly not going to be assisted by the elements.

Plate 1.5
Interior of a Zeppelin control car. The commander of the airship would have had overall authority on a wide range of functions, from target acquisition to bomb type selection and release.

Zeppelin L-3, was commanded by Kapitänleutnant Hans Fritz, along with his executive officer, Leutnant zur See von Lynckner. Zeppelin L-4 fell under the command of Kapitänleutnant Count Magnus von Platen-Hallermund and his executive officer, Leutnant zur See Kruse. Both Zeppelins were stationed at Fuhlsbüttel naval base near Hamburg. Zeppelin L-6 was commanded by Oberleutnant Horst Julius Freiherr Treusch von Buttlar-Brandenfels and was based at the new German Naval Zeppelin headquarters at Nordholz, close to the Lower Saxony coast. Also travelling onboard Zeppelin L-6, was Fregattenkapitän Peter Strasser, Chief of the Imperial German Navy, who would be leading and overseeing the entire raid.

Each commander spent the hours before departure re-running the finer points of their mission plans; plans which had been personally authorised

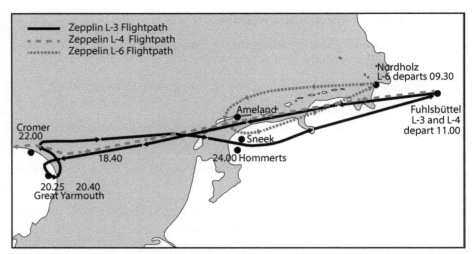

by the Kaiser himself. Zeppelins L-3 and L-4 were to head directly across the North Sea to Humberside, from where they would attack military and industrial targets which formed this vital port. Zeppelin L-6 was to head south towards the Thames estuary and from there attack the prestige industrial and dockland targets but explicitly not the capital itself.

Although not by any means perfect, the weather forecast was deemed satisfactory enough for the raid to proceed. Zeppelin L-6 was the first to leave her hangar at Nordholz at 9.30 a.m. and lift up into the cover of thick cloud. She was then followed by Zeppelins L-3 and L-4 at 11.00 a.m. All airships headed east, crossing the Dutch coast and then across the North Sea to the British mainland. The plan was to use the daylight hours to navigate over the North Sea and then begin their attacks under the cover of darkness.

Shortly after crossing the Dutch coast the raid developed its first problem. Zeppelin L-6, with Strasser onboard, had developed serious mechanical difficulties. The crew's attempts to rectify the problem, a broken crankshaft in one of the engines, proved to be unsuccessful. To continue onwards would mean to risk dropping into the North Sea and an almost certain death, even before they got close to their target. Much to Strasser's immense frustration, the only viable option was turn around and try to make it back to Nordholz. By coaxing its engine, the airship was able to return safely. Although unable to take part on this raid, Zeppelin L-6 was to be involved in later raids, and it was one of these a couple of months later which highlighted the absurd notion of Zeppelin raids precisely finding their targets. On the 15th April, 1915, Zeppelin L-6 was part of another three airship raid to attack Humberside. Instead of dropping its bomb load on the huge industrial port, the airship, again commanded by von Buttlar-Brandenfels, exacted severe damage and panic, but thankfully no casualties, on the town of Maldon in Essex about 200 miles away! Notwithstanding this, von Buttlar-Brandenfels still managed to report that this was a successful raid on Humberside.

As Zeppelin L-6 turned around and limped back across the sea, the remaining two airships were about to receive further bad news. Weather forecasts for the area around Humberside were now predicting very inclement weather and as such the commanders of both airships were forced into a change of plan. Instead of Humberside, new targets were selected along the Norfolk coast.

Darkness had now fallen and the two Zeppelins that had been hovering in position above the cold waves of the North Sea, now began their approach which would take them over mainland Britain for the first time. Zeppelins L-3 and L-4 flew together, taking them over and between the Hasboro and Would lightships; a course that would see them make landfall at a point somewhere between Mundesley and Sea Palling.

The first sighting of the approaching airships was made at 6.40pm by a young man at Ingham, who looking out over the sea saw two 'stars' low over the water. As the Zeppelins came in sight of the Norfolk coastline they separated, Zeppelin L-4 taking a north-westerly course, turning at Bacton at 7.55pm and then flying just inshore and up and around the coast. Meanwhile, Zeppelin L-3 was seen by a patrol of the 6th Battalion, Norfolk Regiment (Cyclists) Territorial Force crossing the coast at 8.05pm, at a point between Eccles-on-Sea and Sea Palling. The airship then turned south-east towards Great Yarmouth, passing over Lessingham, Ingham and Martham.

Zeppelin L-3 commenced its attack at around 8.15pm by dropping a number of parachute flares just above the village of Martham, struggling to gain its bearings and identify a route to Great Yarmouth. The *Yarmouth Mercury* records the recovery of a flare casing close to the hall at Martham the following day. 'The casing was about 2 feet long and 3½ inches in diameter. At one end, which was solid except for a sort of turn screw in the centre, were the figures 6, 12, 15, 18 at even distances round the edge and there were various German words on the tube itself'. The flares, along with the dull throbbing sound of its engines, would have notified the population below of its presence. However, the alarm had already been raised by the crew of the Haisboro lightship, who had also been alerted by the passing engine noise. The authorities in London first received notice of the impending raid just after 8.00pm, just as Zeppelin L-3 was making preparations for its attack.

During many Zeppelin nighttime raids, the inability of the airship's crew to be able to identify their location and gain their bearings was to be a common occurrence. One of the most valuable navigation features for them to pick out were railway lines. Sometimes a clear night would allow them to see moonlight reflecting from the tracks; if they were lucky they would be able to see the firebox from a moving steam locomotive. On the night of the 19th January, breaks in the cloud cover enabled L-3's crew to pick out the North Walsham to Great Yarmouth line, which they followed towards the lights of the Great Yarmouth. Although the authorities in London had just been made aware of an impending raid, no alarm had been passed on to the town's authorities.

Flying at 5,000 feet, Zeppelin L-3 began its attack on the northern outskirts of Great Yarmouth at 8.25pm:

Bomb 1 – The first bomb to be dropped was an incendiary which fell harmlessly into a waterlogged field owned by a local farmer George Humphrey, near St Michael's Church at Little Ormesby. The bomb exploded causing no damage but left a small crater approximately half metre wide.

Bomb 2 – Another incendiary bomb, dropped at 8.25pm and the first to fall on Great Yarmouth itself, exploding in the middle of the lawn of a house at 6, Albemarle Road which belonged to a Mr. Norwood Suffling. No major damage was caused but the bomb left a small crater in the lawn.

Fig. 1.2
Plan of Zeppelin L-3's attack
on Little Ormesby, showing
the location of the incendiary
bomb which fell harmlessly
into a nearby field.

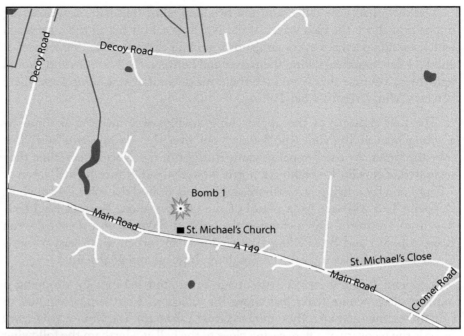

Fig. 1.3
Plan of bombs dropped
by Zeppelin L-3 on Great
Yarmouth during its raid on
the night of 19th January,
1915.

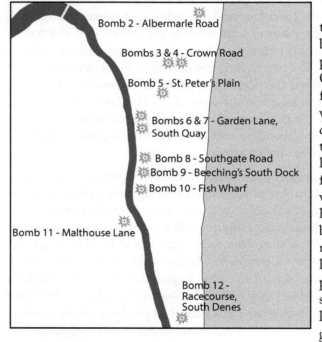

Bomb 3 – The first of the 110lb high explosive bombs, which fell on a pathway to the rear of 78 Crown Road. The bomb failed to explode and was later recovered and defused. The occupant of the house, Mrs. Osborne, had an extremely fortuitous escape. She was just about to enter her back door when the bomb crashed down nearby, narrowly missing her. Speaking to the press the following day, she described it 'it was like a big gun... If I had gone just a step or two further I would have been killed'. The bomb was safely recovered and defused by a team from the Norfolk National Reservists.

Bomb 4 – A further incendiary bomb fell close to Crown Road. It failed to detonate and left a small crater close to livery stables owned by a Mr. W.F. Miller.

Bomb 5 – A high explosive bomb which would claim the lives of the first civilians to be killed in an air raid on the British mainland. The bomb fell on the St. Peter's Plain area of the town, a densely populated area. Miss Martha Taylor, 72 years old, had been returning from the grocers when she was killed. An account of the events of the night describes the harrowing event: 'The scene in St Peter's Plain was one of considerable ruin. Windows were blown out and walls and woodwork shattered in all directions and the roadway covered in considerable debris. At the head of the passage the body of Miss Taylor was found. She was shockingly mangled and most of her clothes were torn off. There was a large wound in the lower part of her body and part of her arm was torn off and lay in the road near her.'

Sam Smith, a 53 year old shoemaker, had gone outside to see what the noise was at the moment the bomb fell upon him. Standing about 30 feet away from the impact point of the bomb, he received a devastating blast of shrapnel that caused an instantaneous death. A further two people suffered injuries.

Many buildings suffered severe damage. Number 25 which was owned by a Mr. Ellis, a fish curer, received a direct hit but he was only slightly injured by flying glass as he was in the back of the house at the time and was saved by a door falling on him which shielded him from much of the blast debris. Several properties that had not been destroyed by the initial explosion subsequently had to be demolished.

Bombs 6 & 7 – Two high explosive bombs fell together on a stable at the

Plate 1.6
Albemarle Road, location of the first incendiary bomb to be dropped on Great Yarmouth during the raid by Zeppelin L-3. The bomb exploded on the lawn of the house at No. 6, causing little damage.

Plate 1.7
Rear of Crown Road, Great Yarmouth, site of another incendiary bomb dropped by Zeppelin L-3. The bomb fell close to livery stables but failed to detonate.

Plate 1.8
Damage caused by the 5th of Zeppelin L-3's bombs, which was dropped on the St. Peter's Plain area of Great Yarmouth. The high explosive bomb killed 70 year old Martha Taylor and 53 year old Sam Smith.

Plate 1.9
The house in St. Peter's Plain which was destroyed by the bomb as it looks today.

Plate 1.10
The blue plaque commemorating the deaths of Samuel Smith and Martha Taylor, killed by the bomb dropped on St. Peter's Plain.

back of butcher William Mays' premises on Green Lane, near South Quay. Both failed to detonate and crashed through the roof of the stable and were found the following morning next to a pony obliviously grazing on its hay. The bombs were recovered and then sunk at sea where they were detonated harmlessly.

Bomb 8 – An incendiary bomb that fell opposite a shop near the First and Last pub on Southgate Road, close to the Fish Wharf. The bomb did not cause any casualties but shattered many of the neighbouring buildings' windows. Many nearby houses were covered in 'some grey substance' which was probably unspent combustible fluid.

Bomb 9 – Using the River Yare as a guide, the Zeppelin moved south across the town to drop a further incendiary bomb which failed to detonate. The bomb fell between two vessels, the drifter *Mishe Nahma* and the pilot boat *Patrol*, crashing against the wooden gates of Beeching's South Dock.

Bomb 10 – A high explosive bomb which landed on ground behind the Fish Wharf, its impact making a large crater. The explosion damaged a nearby water tower, ruptured the water mains and destroyed a lamp standard. The blast shattered the glass roof of the wharf and wrecked an adjacent restaurant and office building. Fortunately only one person, the Fish Wharf master, Captain Smith, was injured by flying glass. At a meeting of the Yarmouth Port and Haven Commission the following day, the resident engineer estimated that the cost of the damage caused by the raid was between £500 and £600. The herring fleet which would normally have been moored near to the Fish Wharf had fortuitously been moved up river just two days prior to the raid.

Bomb 11 – Another high explosive bomb, which fell next to the steam drifter *Piscatorial*. The boat was owned by the unfortunate Harry Eastick, who had already lost one boat in the war to a mine. Shrapnel from the blast also

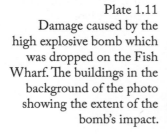

Plate 1.11
Damage caused by the high explosive bomb which was dropped on the Fish Wharf. The buildings in the background of the photo showing the extent of the bomb's impact.

damaged a grain store on Malthouse Lane, owned by Coombe and Co.

Bomb 12 – The final bomb to fall was another high explosive munition, falling behind the racecourse at South Denes, just under a mile away from the previous bomb. This caused a large crater but apart from blowing over a fence, very little other structural damage was incurred.

Plate 1.12
Evidence of the shrapnel damage caused by another high explosive bomb which was dropped close to the steam drifter *Piscatorial*.

The raid over Yarmouth had barely taken ten minutes. With her payload of munitions successfully delivered, Kapitänleutnant Hans Fritz gave orders for the airship to head out to sea. Looking back he would see the lights of the town being belatedly extinguished under the orders of the Borough Engineer. Once safely out over the sea, Zeppelin L-3 turned back up and along the coast, arriving offshore near Cromer around 10.00pm. From here it turned north east and headed for home. Between midnight and 1.00am the residents of the northern Dutch towns of Sneek and Hommerts heard the airship passing overheard on its way back to its base in Fuhlsbüttel.

All members of the crews of Zeppelins L-3 and L-4 were to be decorated by the Kaiser with Iron Crosses for their part in the raids. The airship and its crew did not have long to bask in the glory of their successful blitz. Less than a month later Zeppelin L-3's wartime exploits would come to an end. A forced landing during a heavy snow storm on the Danish island of Fanø saw the airship destroyed, eleven crew interred and four reported as missing.

Back in Great Yarmouth, the dawn of the new day broke to find the town's residents still in a state of shock from the previous night's events. Crowds gathered to view the grim results that the German bombs had wrought and soon news of the casualties inflicted had spread across the town. As more people saw the destroyed buildings, strewn rubble and shattered windows, the mood of the population turned from one of shock to one of anger. How had a German Zeppelin been able to cross the North Sea and then unchallenged, fly over land and bomb innocent civilian targets without any response from British forces? The residents' anger was also directed at the authorities who had given no warning of the raid.

The raid not only made local and national news but was also covered internationally. As would be expected during wartime, local and national media largely downplayed the damage caused by the raid, the main focus being to denounce the Germans for their underhand tactics of bombing civilian targets. On the other side of the North Sea, the raid obviously brought a totally different reaction. In Germany the mood was one of triumph. On Wednesday 20th January, Reuters in Amsterdam reported that an official telegram had been received from Berlin:

'On the night of January 19, naval airships undertook an attack on some fortified places on the English coast. The weather was foggy and rainy. Several bombs were successfully dropped. The airships were shot at but returned unhurt. Deputy Chief of the Admiralty, von Behnke'.

On the same day, a report in the Exchange Special in Amsterdam described the reaction of the German population to the news of the raid:

'Reports here this afternoon from Berlin state that the news of the Zeppelin raid on East Anglia has caused the wildest delight and satisfaction throughout Germany.

It is stated that the raid had been planned for months past, and only awaited the opportunity for its accomplishment. It is also stated that 'it is only a beginning'.

Newspaper comment is eulogistic, and runs on the lines that German genius has at last ended the legend that England was invulnerable owing to her insularity.

The rumour published in England to the effect that one of the Zeppelins has been brought down is not mentioned in any of the messages from Berlin, but at noon none of the airships had returned to their bases'.

In America, the raid drew savage criticism for its attack on innocent civilian targets. The *New York Herald* ran an editorial titled 'More Slaughter of Innocents' on the 20th January:

'Is it the madness of despair or just plain madness that prompted the Germans to select for attack peaceful undefended resorts on England's East Coast? What can Germany hope to gain from these wanton attacks on undefended places and the slaughter of innocents? Certainly not the good opinion of the peoples of the neutral nations, for these know that the rules of civilised warfare call for notice of bombardment even of places fortified and defended'.

The *New York Tribune* described the raid as a 'disgrace to civilisation' and having but one purpose; 'a desire to terrorise England and raise a cheer in the streets of Berlin. A wanton and brutal disregard for The Hague rules and humane principles, the raid belongs with the worst acts of German militarism in the present war'.

However, not all sections of the American press were quite as condemnatory in their tone. The pro-German *Milwaukee Free Press* headlined its 20th January front page with 'Zeppelins bombard Sandringham. As King George and the Queen flee, panic grips the capital as foe steers course for London'.

Outrage at the fact that the Germans had chosen to attack innocent civilian targets was the lead in most British national newspapers. The *Daily Mirror* ran the headline 'The Coming of the Baby Killers'; a term that would picked up and used to describe the Zeppelins throughout the rest of their campaign against British mainland targets. The rest of the *Daily Mirror's* article focused on the German's callous disregard for taking the lives of ordinary citizens:

'Germany was overjoyed by the news of its 'gallant' air huns' murder raid. Its peoples' joy at the success of the Zeppelin attack was widely enthusiastic. I have an intuitive feeling that the joy could not have been greater even if Dr. Barnardo's Homes had been destroyed'.

The inquests into the death of Miss Taylor and Mr Smith were held on the afternoon of 21st January, 1915. The jury returning a verdict that both deaths had been caused by the explosion of a bomb dropped from a hostile aircraft. The Borough coroner, Mr J. T. Waters, stated that the deaths were 'the wanton killing of harmless people and were nothing short of murder".

Chapter 2

The Zeppelin L-4 Raid

While Zeppelin L-3 was making a south easterly course after crossing the coast near Bacton, at 7.55pm her sister airship on the 19th January, 1915 raid, Zeppelin L-4, was turning in a north easterly direction; heading up and around the coastline towards The Wash.

Built at Friedrichshafen, Zeppelin L-4 (factory designation LZ-27) was 518 feet, 2 inches in length and its 18 gas cells had a combined volume of 794,500 cubic feet. Its three engines giving it a trial speed of 51.4 mph, a not insignificant speed for the time. The airship carried a crew of 16 men, commanded by Kapitänleutnant Count Magnus von Platen-Hallermund and had left its base at Fuhlsbüttel carrying an armament payload of eight 110lb high explosive bombs and ten incendiary bombs.

Flying low a little way inland, Zeppelin L-4 passed over Mundesley and the coastal villages of Sidestrand and Overstrand before arriving on the outskirts of Cromer shortly before 8.30pm. A warning had already been received in the town of the raid that was currently taking place along the coast at Great Yarmouth. Lights were already being extinguished to make identification from above a much harder task for the Zeppelin crew. Perhaps it was because of this that some Cromer residents who had ventured out into the streets described the airship as circling extremely low over the town. The Zeppelin crew appeared to be unsure of their bearings and in a few minutes the craft had headed out over the sea again, travelling further north up the coast.

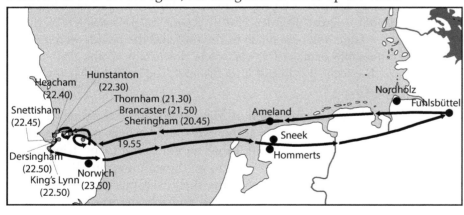

Fig. 2.1
Flightpath of Zeppelin L-4 for its raid on various locations in West Norfolk during the night of 19th January, 1915.

Five minutes later the airship had reached Sheringham where it looped back inland, descending to about 800 feet. This time Zeppelin L-4's commander, von Platen-Hallermund ordered a flare to be dropped to help him locate his position. At 8.45pm, moving over the centre of town the airship commenced its attack:

Bomb 1 – Zeppelin L-4's first bomb of the raid was an incendiary bomb which fell on a house in Jordan's Yard, off Wyndham Street. The owner, a bricklayer Robert Smith, was in the house with his wife and daughter when the bomb crashed through the roof, through the bedroom and kitchen ceilings, before finally embedding itself in the floor of the kitchen without exploding. The bomb caused considerable damage to the house but all its occupants escaped serious injury. The noise from the bomb hitting the building brought many neighbours out to see what had happened; one of them subsequently picked up the bomb and calmly placed it a bucket before taking it away.

Fig. 2.2
Plan showing
locations of incendiary
bombs dropped on
Sheringham by
Zeppelin L-4.

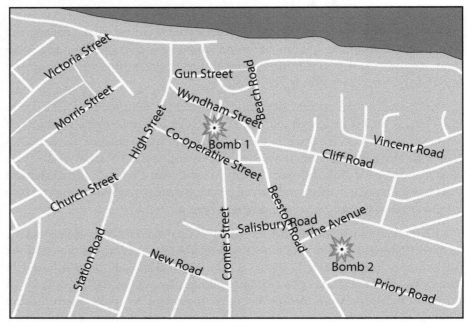

The *Cromer and North Norfolk Post* described the Smith family's experience:

'The chair in which she was sitting was slightly damaged. The family were naturally terrified. Our representative who visited the house found the bedroom in great disorder. Hardly a pane of glass was left in the windows, a large hole was made in the roof and the boards were torn up. Considerable damage was also done downstairs to the floor and furniture. The scene was one of utter disorder. The landlord, Mr Jordan, is not insured.

Another little girl, a companion of May Smith who was sitting in the same room, received an injury to her wrist and her hair was singed. 'I never had such a fright in my life. I shall never forget it to my dying day' remarked Mrs Smith, 'I never want to go through it again.' The bomb was about 4½ inches in diameter. The shell itself must have weighed about twelve pounds. If it had exploded probably the whole square of houses would have been wrecked and lives lost. Mr Smith, the occupier of the house, said 'It all came so suddenly. The bomb fell near the fireplace and it is a wonder how we escaped serious injury. My impression is that it was a fire-ball and that the object of the raiders was to burn the houses.'

Bomb 2 – The next bomb, another incendiary, fell a few minutes later. Landing on open ground near The Avenue and Priory Road, it exploded leaving a small crater, causing no injuries or damage. The dropping of the bomb was observed by a police inspector who was on duty in Cromer Road, located to the south of the incident. He rushed back to his station to telephone warnings to other towns. Zeppelin L-4 had completed its attack on Sheringham and swung back out sea. Passing Wells-next-the-Sea, it was now about 15 miles offshore and looking to the west, its crew would

Plate 2.1
Blue plaque commemorating the dropping of the first of Zeppelin L-4's bombs on a house in Jordan's Yard, Sheringham. Although the bomb failed to explode, it caused considerable damage to the house but did not cause serious injury to its occupants.

have seen the lights of Skegness shining in the distance but von Platen-Hallermund gave orders to head back towards the Norfolk coast.

Bomb 3 - Coming in low over the village of Thornham at 9.30pm, the drone of the airship's engines caused villagers to run out of their homes and looking up they could see the faces of the German crew looking down at them

from the control car as the enormous Zeppelin flew over, almost clipping the spire of the school building. An incendiary bomb was dropped on The Green, at the northern edge of the village. L-4 then carried on in an easterly direction for three miles until it arrived at Brancaster village.

Plate 2.2
The Green, Thornham. Location of the incendiary bomb dropped by Zeppelin L-4.

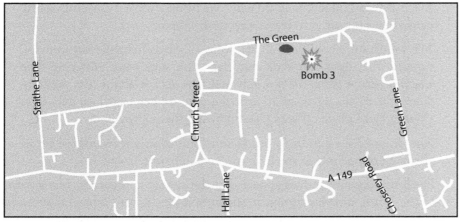

Fig. 2.3
Plan showing locations of incendiary bomb dropped on Thornham by Zeppelin L-4.

Bomb 4 - Another incendiary, this bomb fell in the road on Broad Lane, Brancaster at 9.50pm. Zeppelin L-4 had circled the village three times, intermittently hovering. The first of these circuits being the largest with the drone of the engines picked up at Stanhoe and Docking. On its third circuit the incendiary bomb was released, falling at the base of a triangle comprising Brancaster church, the Dormy House Club and a house belonging to Mr W.H. Game. As the bomb exploded, the airship turned on its searchlight and it could be clearly seen against the night sky by those residents who had ventured outside. Several others took refuge in the cellar of the Ship Hotel. The bomb did not do any substantial damage, apart from making a small crater about six inches deep. The following morning many of the villagers were eagerly searching for fragments of the bomb to be used as trophies. One of the pieces found bore a large inscription, printed in German 'Warnung' (warning).

Fig. 2.4
Plan of Brancaster, showing location of incendiary bomb dropped by Zeppelin L-4.

Plate 2.3
Broad Lane, Brancaster (looking north), the location of another incendiary bomb dropped by Zeppelin L-4.

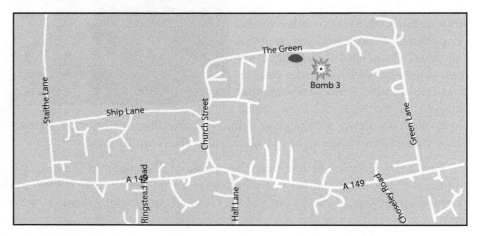

Bomb 5 – From Brancaster, Zeppelin L-4 cut back across land heading towards Hunstanton. There are some contradictions as to when the airship was first sighted over the town, some putting it at 10.15pm, others at 10.30pm. Faced for the first time with a frightening new technology appearing out of the night sky, it is understandable that confusion abounded. An article in the 20th January, 1915 edition of the *Daily Mail* gives an account given by a Mr Barrett, the deputy town clerk of King's Lynn, who was present at the time of the Zeppelin's arrival over Hunstanton:

> 'I was in the Hunstanton Club which is on the Promenade, facing the sea. A rubber had just finished when we heard a terrific noise, obviously caused by a big aircraft. It was exactly 10.30pm.
>
> We went out. I could see a great dim shape against the sky, moving rapidly. The night was dark but clear; the stars were glittering. The machine came from the sea, hovered over us for about five minutes, went out to sea again as if to make sure of her bearings, and then returned and made off very fast, following the railway line.
>
> She dropped no bombs in our vicinity, but soon afterwards we heard the bang of one which she had thrown some miles away'.

From this account it does appear that the airship approached Hunstanton from The Wash and was trying to orientate itself. If von Platen-Hallermund had been aware of his location, by no means a foregone conclusion, he would almost certainly have been able to identify it as Hunstanton. Barely a mile away from the Promenade where Mr Barrett saw Zeppelin L-4 pass over his head was what was known to the locals as 'Hippisley's Hut'; a wireless listening station that was located next to the lighthouse on the distinctive chalk cliffs, overlooking The Wash. The station's operation will be more closely studied in a following chapter but it played an important role in capturing wireless intelligence throughout the war. Although the function and location of such stations was supposed to be a closely guarded secret by British Intelligence, they had in fact allowed a comprehensive and revealing article to be published in a pre-war issue of *Electrical Engineering*!

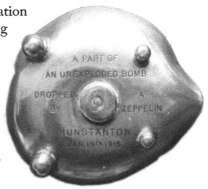

Only a single high explosive bomb was dropped, landing in a field adjacent to what is now the A149 road, about 300 yards away from the wireless station. The bomb did not explode (giving support to locals believing that no bombs had been dropped as the Zeppelin passed overhead) and was later recovered.

Bomb 6 – Zeppelin L-4 left Hunstanton and using the railway line as a guide, headed south towards King's Lynn. By 10.40pm it had reached Heacham, where it circled overhead before swooping across the village to discharge its next bomb. This was an incendiary, falling on a cottage in Lord's Lane, owned by a Mrs Patrick. A witness to this was a Captain Neville-Rolfe, who having been wounded at the Front the previous month, was recovering back home in the village:

'Towards the end of January I was woken one night by what sounded like twenty motorcycles charging down a neighbouring hill, but proved to be the first Zeppelin raid on England. The airship, flying very low, crossed coast at our village, giving Heacham the distinction of receiving the first bomb ever dropped on English soil. It was an incendiary and appropriately dropped in a washerwoman's soft water butt. What she said about 'them there Jarmans' might have stopped the war had the Kaiser heard it. The second bomb was a 50 kilo high explosive which did not explode'.

Plate 2.5
Lord's Lane, Heacham. An incendiary bomb was dropped on a cottage, causing minimal damage.

Another resident, Mr R. Pull, said that he had gone to bed at around 10.15pm when he heard what he thought was an aeroplane and then the noise of the first bomb exploding:

'There was a flash and an explosion and a tremendous noise which increased in volume. After the explosion I immediately called out "Put all lights out" and got down the stairs and ran to one of the neighbours and extinguished theirs. I went to another for the same purpose as the airship seemed to be returning. A minute or two later the windows rattled from the effect of another explosion, possibly that at Snettisham'.

Apart from tearing away some roof tiles and demolishing the water butt, no damage was caused or injuries sustained.

Bomb 7 – The second bomb to fall on Heacham came down in a field, owned by a Mr Brasnett, located between the old village school and the chalk pit on the eastern side of the A149 road. The 100lb high explosive bomb did not explode and was only discovered two days later by a boy who happened to be walking across the field. The authorities were alerted and soldiers of the 1/1st Lincolnshire Yeomanry, who were stationed in the village at the time, recovered the bomb and transported it to Homemead on Hunstanton Road, where the unit's officers were billeted. The bomb was put under guard but placed on display to the villagers until it was collected by officers from Woolwich Arsenal for further examination.

Plate 2.6
The high explosive bomb which fell in a field to the east of the A149 at Heacham but failed to explode. The bomb was put on public display until recovery by officers from Woolwich Arsenal.

Bomb 8 – From Heacham, Zeppelin L-4 moved eastwards inland towards Sedgeford before it turned south west, arriving at Snettisham around 10.45pm. Once over the village it headed towards St. Mary's Church where one of the more controversial incidents of the raid took place. St. Mary's Church was described by Professor Sir Nikolaus Pevsner as being 'the most exciting 14th century decorated church in Norfolk'. Its 175 ft. high tower and spire was often a landmark for mariners navigating The Wash and was known as one of the three spires of Norfolk. It would have proved a distinctive landmark for the airship's crew. As the Zeppelin cruised over the village, residents looked up at its sinister darkened shape, flying so low that the interior lights of the cabin could be seen through the gondola's trapdoor that had opened in preparation for releasing its bombs.

An account of the ensuing events was later collated by the vicar of St. Mary's, the Rev. Ilsely W. Charlton:

> 'Supposing that the distant noise was the hum of an ordinary aeroplane, and that some lights would be visible, my wife and I and a lady friend were walking about in the garden, trying to penetrate the darkness and discover the aircraft. The drone of the engine was so much louder than usual that we were quite prepared to descry at length, exactly overhead, the outline of a Zeppelin hovering over the church and vicarage at a great height, appearing at a distance, to be only about fifteen or twenty yards long.

> No sooner had we identified it as probably a German airship, that suddenly all doubt was dispelled by a long, loud hissing sound; a confused streak of light and a tremendous crash. The next moment was made up of apprehension, relief and mutual enquiries, and then all was dark and still, as the sound of the retiring Zeppelin speedily died away'.

The airship was first seen hovering over the old Grammar School, which stood at the bottom of the hill leading out of the village. It appeared to be leaving the village towards Inmere, passing to the left of the church but hovered over the houses on the edge of the village before turning back. It circled St. Mary's church twice before a tremendous explosion reverberated across the village, shattering many windows of nearby houses. The church itself suffered the worst of the damage with twenty two of its windows being smashed. One window in the vestry was completely blown in but the nearby organ escaped any damage. The bomb that had fallen was yet another high explosive, landing in a small meadow

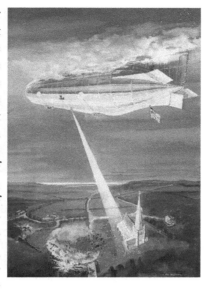

Plate 2.7
Illustration of Zeppelin L-4 illuminating St. Mary's church, Snettisham and releasing the high explosive bomb which exploded in the meadow opposite the church.

owned by Mr Coleridge, four yards from Sedgeford Road; the wet ground of the field and the surrounding stone walls lessening the effect of the explosion.

Why the church was specifically targeted remains a mystery, although this did not stop some national newspapers from professing their own ideas; a *Daily Mail* article scornfully suggesting that 'No German airman can resist a church'.

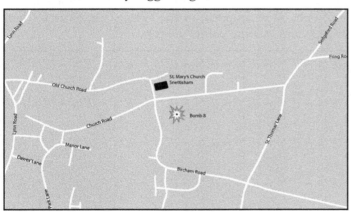

Rumours were rife following the raid that the airship was in fact trying to locate Sandringham, where King George V had in fact been staying up until the 18th January. Such stories had no basis. All

Fig. 2.5
Plan of the bomb which was dropped close to St. Mary's Church, Snettisham.

Zeppelin crews were fully aware of the Kaiser's explicit orders that no palaces or residences of the British royal family were to be attacked. However, this did not stop the *Hamburger Nachrichten* pushing the boundaries of the Kaiser's edict with their summary of the night's events

'On the way to King's Lynn, Sandringham, the present residence of King George was not overlooked. Bombs fell in the neighbourhood of Sandringham and a loud crash notified the King of England that the Germans were not

Plate 2.8
The windows of St. Mary's Church, Snettisham being boarded up after having been shattered by the blast of the explosive bomb which fell nearby.

Plate 2.9
St. Mary's church,
Snettisham. The high
explosive bomb dropped
by Zeppelin L-4 fell in the
field in the lower right of the
photograph.

far off…Our Zeppelins have shown that they could find the hidden royal residence. In any case, they did not intend to hit it, and only gave an audible notification of their presence in the immediate neighbourhood.'

After dropping its single bomb on Snettisham the airship briefly switched on its searchlight to scour the scene below before it headed off south in the direction of Dersingham. By now local authorities were beginning to receive news from frightened members of the public of the ongoing raids. As Zeppelin L-4 passed over Dersingham at about 10.45pm, the local police superintendent made a phone call to the Chief Constable of King's Lynn, Charles Hunt, to forewarn him of the impending arrival of the airship. Before they had finished their conversation, Hunt later recounted that he 'heard bombs being dropped close to the borough'.

Bomb 9 – A lesser recorded event appears to have taken place before the airship left Dersingham. A resident of the village, Cliff Riches, who was only four years old at the time later recounted the incident: 'the Zeppelin came over my house from the direction of the sea and that the first bomb fell in what is now Manorside but was then a field'. There are later accounts of a Zeppelin raid in 1916, where bombs were dropped on the village. Accounts for both events appear incomplete and at some points overlap.

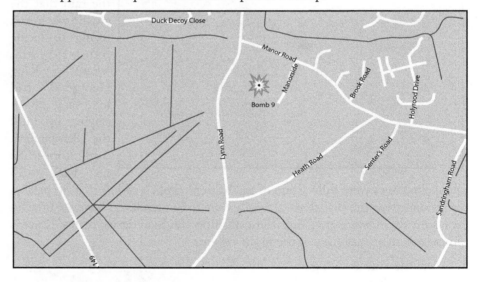

Fig. 2.6
Plan of the location of the putative bomb dropped in the field in what is today, Manorside, Dersingham.

Bomb 10 – By 22.50pm Zeppelin L-4 had reached the parish of Gaywood on the eastern side of King's Lynn. As he approached the town, von Platen-Hallermund would have seen its street lights still shining brightly below. The airship was still flying low at this point, with some accounts have her flying as low as 300 feet. On immediately hearing the sound of nearby explosions, Chief Constable Hunt ordered the Borough Electrical Engineer to turn off all street and residential lighting but this order was issued too late to hide the town from the airship's view. An account of its arrival over King's Lynn was given by a Mr Harold Baldock, a clerk at the police station:

'I was at home finishing a letter. At about ten minutes to eleven I heard two sounds, which coming together, aroused my suspicions.

One was an unusual rattling of windows, the other a peculiar barking by my spaniel. Now, when I was stationed at Lincoln and Mr Hucks used to fly there, the spaniel always barked like that when he heard his machine - then and at no other time. I went out. I heard a dull buzzing noise, which rapidly became louder. I saw nothing at first, for the night, though clear and starry, was pitch dark. Then I picked out a great big cigar-shaped airship, flying low and fast. The hospital was partly lit up and a conspicuous sight. The Zeppelin seemed to make that her centre and to fly round and round the town.

She carried no light. I saw her drop four bombs; twice I felt a sort of shaking of the air which suggested that she had dropped two more. The bombs dropped like shooting stars. They made a reddish, yellowish light as they fell - probably the fuse; a glare was reflected in the sky when they burst. The first bomb fell at four minutes to eleven, the last at three minutes past eleven. Then the airship made off over the Wash, going back the way that she came'.

Plate 2.10
Manorside, Dersingham. Location of a further bomb dropped by Zeppelin L-4 during its raid on the night of 19th January, 1915.

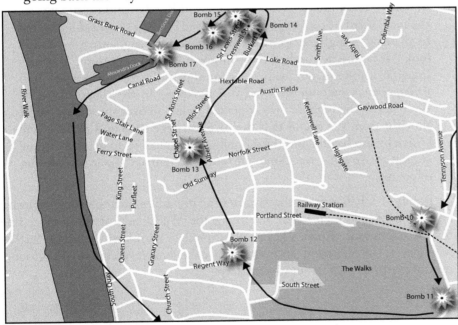

Fig. 2.7
Map of the locations where bombs were dropped on King's Lynn by Zeppelin L-4.

The first bomb to be dropped on King's Lynn was a high explosive bomb, falling in a field adjoining the Hunstanton railway line behind Tennyson Avenue. The bomb exploded, breaking a number of windows in nearby houses in Tennyson Avenue and Park Avenue but caused no casualties.

A resident of Tennyson Avenue described how he thought the approaching Zeppelin was in fact a railway engine:

'I went to the back door and I saw a flash and before I could turn to go back nearly the whole of the back windows of the house were blown in. A bomb had fallen in a field about 100 yards from the back of the house and there is a big hole in the ground. All the windows in this part of the Avenue seem to have suffered in the same way. I went to the front of the house and saw two more flashes. My neighbours on one side have their windows broken worse than mine'.

Another resident of Tennyson Avenue, Mr R. Doyly Watkins described the explosion:

'I was standing in the garden and one piece of turf grazed my shoulder. All the windows in the back of the house went at the same moment. Then a bomb went in front of the house in the allotments near the railway station. There was a greyish-blue flash'.

The Inspector of King's Lynn railway station, Mr R. Woodbine, later wrote of his experiences on the night of the raid in a letter to the Lynn News

'I had arrived in our junction signal box just before the first bomb fell. The signalman had told me he noticed a distant report which had shaken his windows and looking out of his box windows I heard a noise resembling an aeroplane. I remarked, as the noise grew in volume, that is no Britisher and told him to put his lights down as the visitor was evidently coming for us. He also told Exton's Road signalman to do the same. The noise seemed in a direct line with the signal box coming from the direction of the Ship Inn on Gaywood Road. I could distinctly see the movement of the propeller but not the body of the machine owing to it being straight in front of me. I called the signalman to have a look but before he reached the window the first crash came. You may imagine, if you can, our feelings. I cannot describe them and never wish to experience such another fright. I remained in the signal box until three bombs had fallen; they appeared to fall all over the station and I thought from the sound that the royal carriage shed and station were struck by the second and third bombs. I was anxious to get back to the station to see what was done but found no damage to either building of course.'

Bomb 11 – Falling very shortly after the preceding one, this high explosive bomb fell on allotments that ran along the Walks side of the railway line towards Tennyson Road. The bomb exploded harmlessly, causing further windows to be shattered and leaving a considerable crater in the ground, measuring 16 feet across and 7 feet deep.

Plate 2.11
Troops posing for a photograph in the crater left by the eleventh of L-4's bombs, a 110lb high explosive 'bomb, which fell in a field adjoining the Hunstanton railway line behind Tennyson Avenue, King's Lynn.

EAST COAST AIR RAID JAN 19th 1915.
A Hole 17'6" wide, near Royal Train shelter, Lynn Station.

Bomb 12 – This was first bomb to cause fatalities in King's Lynn. The high explosive bomb fell on Bentinck Street, to the rear of St. James' Road, a densely packed area of Victorian terraced houses. The house which took the direct hit from the bomb, 12 Bentinck Street, was the home of John Goate who lived there with his wife and two children; Percy aged fourteen years old and Ethel aged four. The explosion also wrecked the adjoining cottage, number 11, as well. Unfortunately the bomb took the life of Percy Goate. His mother later described the fateful scene:

'We were all upstairs: me, my husband, the baby and Percy, when I heard a buzzing noise. My husband put out the lamp. Then I saw the bomb drop through the skylight and strike the bed where the boy was lying. I tried to wake him but he was dead. Then the house fell. I do not remember any more'.

All members of the household were buried under a pile of rubble of what remained of their house. A rescue party was quickly on the scene and they worked frantically to move the masonry and woodwork to reach those trapped below. Mr Goate was found first, pinned beneath an iron bedstead; he told the rescuers to look for his wife and children. He was eventually freed, along with his wife and daughter; suffering from cuts and abrasions and they were taken to hospital. Unfortunately Percy had died instantly.

Plate 2.12
The devastated buildings in Bentinck Street, King's Lynn, destroyed by a high explosive bomb which killed Alice Gazely and Percy Goate.

Next door at number 11 Bentinck Street, the home of Mr and Mrs Fayers, there was a similar scene of devastation. The Fayers had been joined at their home on the first sign of the bombardment by a Mrs Alice Gazely who lived nearby and who had sought refuge there. Alice Gazely had recently been widowed, her husband having been killed at the Front, and had only just moved back to King's Lynn. The Fayers, buried under the debris of what used to be their house, were eventually freed and transported to hospital but no trace could be found of anyone else. Alice Gazely's sister later remembered the night of the raid:

'It was between 10 and 11 at night when the Zeppelin came over. It made a zooming noise and then the next thing we heard was this bang. They had had word in the town that they were over at Yarmouth and they phoned through to the police but they didn't take any notice of it and their lights were still all on. But when the bang came, the lights all went off.

My father didn't know where my sister was but she had been killed. He hunted all around in the pitch black, it was so dark you couldn't see a thing. Eventually he found out she was in this house where people had been taken to the hospital but nothing was done to find her until the morning. My father went and found her and dug her out'.

Mr Henry Rowe, Alice Gazely's father, had last seen his daughter about 10.00pm, shortly before the raid began. After hearing the noise of the first bombs dropping, he went back to his daughter's house but was unable to find her. Returning at 7.00am the following morning, he found Mrs Fayers who told him that she had been having some supper with his daughter when the bombs began to fall. As the noise of the Zeppelin's engines grew louder, Alice cried 'There's a dreadful noise. Oh good God, what is it?'. With that she rushed outside into the street, just as the first bomb exploded.

Plate 2.13
Front page of the *Daily Mirror*, Thursday 21st January 1915. The article highlights the scenes of devastation caused by Zeppelin L-4's raid on King's Lynn. The epithet 'Baby Killers' would become a commonly used term to refer to the German Zeppelin crews.

Bomb 13 – The next bomb fell at the corner of East Street and Albert Avenue. The bomb exploded to the rear of a property owned by a blacksmith, Mr T. H. Walden, destroying his workshop and causing considerable damage to the surrounding houses. Many people had to be rescued from the debris of their demolished homes but miraculously none suffered serious injury.

Plate 2.14
Albert Avenue, King's Lynn. The location of where another 110lb high explosive bomb was dropped nearby, causing considerable damage to surrounding buildings.

Bomb 14 – Was an incendiary bomb which fell on 63 Cresswell Street, where a Mr J.C. Savage lived with his family. The bomb smashed through the roof of the house. It then crashed into a bedroom, piercing a tin box which contained the treasures of their son who had gone to war. It passed through the bedroom floor before embedding itself in the stone floor of the kitchen. It appears that the fuse broke off the device and fell into the neighbouring yard, ensuring further damage was avoided. Remarkably no injuries were suffered.

Plate 2.15
63 Cresswell Street, King's Lynn. An incendiary bomb was dropped, crashing through the roof of the property but failed to detonate.

Bomb 15 – A high explosive bomb which fell on an allotment near Sir Lewis Street. The explosion made a crater 15 feet across and demolished nearby fences and trees but no injuries were sustained by the blast.

Plate 2.16
Sir Lewis Street, King's Lynn. A high explosive bomb was dropped on a nearby allotment. The detonation caused minimal damage and no injuries.

Bomb 16 – Fell in the back garden of a house, owned by Mr Kerner Greenwood, close to the docks and failed to explode.

Bomb 17 – A high explosive bomb which fell on the power station at King's Lynn docks. The explosion destroyed two of the boilers and also wrecked the hydraulic

Plate 2.17
The site close to Alexandra Dock, King's Lynn, where a high-explosive bomb fell on the power station and damaged the lock gate's hydraulic gear.

gear which operated the Alexandra Dock gates. Jack Leader was working nearby when the bomb hit the power station:

> 'When the ship came over, it was a huge thing, like a long sausage. It had boats underneath it. And it seemed as though you could see the heads of the people that were in it. As they made towards the docks, I got on my bike with several others and cycled over to put the lights out'.

The raid on King's Lynn had taken just over ten minutes and with her payload reduced, Zeppelin L-4 turned east, leaving the town below in shock. The airship passed over Grimston, before tracking back over Gayton and West Acre, reaching Dereham at 11.35pm. It then skirted Norwich around 11.50 p.m. before flying out over the sea near Great Yarmouth at 12.30. At 12.45 p.m., von Platen-Hallermund radioed his attack report 'Successfully bombed fortified places between the Tyne and Humber'.

When military officers surveyed the results of the damage caused by the raid the following morning they seemed amazed by the fact that so much damage that had been caused by the Zeppelin's bombs. One was heard to remark 'how could a small bomb, the size of two cocoa tins, demolish two cottages so completely that all is left of them is a heap of broken bricks and shattered windows'.

In addition to the deaths of Percy Goate and Alice Gazely, the list of those injured who were treated at the hospital read:

> Mr Goate - cut face and swollen ankle.
> Mrs Goate - leg damaged.
> Ethel Goate - aged 4 years, stunned.
> Mr Fayers - cut on head.
> Mrs Fayers - cut on face
> G. Hanson - back of hand cut by glass.
> D. Skipper - face and head cut.
> Mrs Skipper - injured leg.
> G. Parlett - forehead cut and head wound.
> R. Wykes - cut head.
> G.W. Clarke - cut lips.
> W. Anderson - wrist lacerated.

In Charles Hunt's (the Chief Constable of King's Lynn) report on the raid, he outlined the speed with which the raid had taken place

> I at once communicated with Major Astley, who is in charge of the National Guard in the town, also the Officer Commanding the Worcestershire Yeomanry who are billeted here. About 10.45 p.m. when I was trying to get through to Dersingham, the Superintendent there rang me up and stated that a Zeppelin had passed over Dersingham and had dropped bombs in that neighbourhood. Before a message was complete I heard bombs being dropped close to the Borough. Immediately on hearing these explosions the Electrical Engineer put out all lights by switching off at the main, not only putting out lights in the street but in private residences as well. The aircraft was soon over our building and several bomb explosions were heard almost immediately.

A further account of the raid is given in a report written the following day by Major L.E. Darell of the 1st Mounted Brigade, based at nearby Middleton Hall:

'Air raid on King's Lynn and the vicinity

In reference to your telephonic communication of early this morning and my telegram W.150, I beg to report as follows:

A German air raid took place over King's Lynn at 10.55 p.m. last evening, the 19th instant.

(1) at 9.15 p.m. Headquarters, Warwick Yeomanry rang up on the telephone, and reported that a coastguard station had sighted two Zeppelins moving towards Norwich, and in King's Lynn at 9.45 p.m. the Chief Constable was informed that Great Yarmouth had been raided. He at once got in touch with the Chief Electrician, and warned him that the lights must be put out all over the town, which he did.

At 10.55 p.m., the Commanding Officer of the Worcester Yeomanry (Major W. Wiggins) heard one Zeppelin overhead, and five bombs were rapidly dropped in different parts of the town, one in the cemetery and one in each of the following places – East Street, Bentinck Street, Albert Street and the Engine House in the Docks. He at once ordered the regiment to turn out, and they fell in on their Troop Alarm Posts, and accompanied by the Chief Constable, he went round to all the places affected, and finding a fire at one, the Troops assisted in subduing it. They also helped to extricate a man who was buried in a Norfolk Street house, and posts were placed at different places where shop windows had been blown in.

The Regimental Doctor, with his orderlies, also performed good work in minor injuries, many having been cut by glass.

No panic occurred whatsoever, and all the populace showed great presence of mind.

The casualties (all civilians) were as follows –

2 Dead (1 woman and 1 boy)

Detained in Hospital 4

Visiting Hospital 7

The damage done was the total demolition of some five houses, serious damage to others, and a great many windows broken, doors blown down, and the total wreckage of the Hydraulic Power Station in the Dockyard.

(2) From Hunstanton a Zeppelin is reported to have passed over there at 10.40 p.m., flying inland, and estimated at 700 feet up. After 15 minutes it returned but no bombs were thrown.

(3) At Heacham, one bomb was thrown as it passed over, striking the side of a house and glancing off into a water barrel, no damage done.

At the inquest into the two deaths of Alice Gazely and Percy Goate, Dr. G.R. Chadwick giving evidence, said that Percy Goate had a lacerated wound on his nose, along with wounds to the face and breast. He did not think that the wounds were sufficient to account for death, which in his opinion was due to shock. Alice Gazely had several bruises to her face but her death had resulted from shock.'

Mr Raikes, the Recorder of King's Lynn, said:

'It was hard to talk of peace when the blood of innocent victims reddened the very stones of King's Lynn, where murder, dastardly, cruel murder, under the cover of dark, had been brought about. The only defences against such raids was to end the war. Another million men now would in the Autumn make an army against which no Continental Power could stand.'

The inquest into the deaths of Alice Gazely and Percy Goate returned a verdict that they met their deaths by 'an act of the King's enemies'. When the Coroner had recorded the verdict, the jury foreman rose to say that some of the jury members believed that the verdict should be murder. The Deputy Coroner replied that 'that unquestionably all war is murder but for the purpose of an inquest it would almost be adding something, absolutely true I grant you, but hardly necessary. I sympathise heartily with what you say'. The inquest lasted three quarters of an hour and no comment was made upon the circumstances of the raid.

Zeppelin L-4 returned home safely to its base the following day to share, along with its sister ship Zeppelin L-3, in the euphoric praise of the German nation. The Commander of L-4, von Platen-Hallermund's, initial account of the raid gives an enlightening insight into the levels of confusion encountered by Zeppelin crews during these early raids on Britain in trying to actually determine where they were. On crossing the Norfolk coastline near Bacton, von Platen-Hallermund was around 80 miles to the south of his intended target of the industrial area of the Humber! After passing low over Cromer to try and get his bearings, he recalled

'I turned off north, in order to get behind the sea front and to reach and attack the Humber industrial area from the land side. Against expectations, I did not find the north bank of the Humber on a north west course'.

In his account he refers to coming under fire from the ground and releasing explosive bombs in return. By the time the lights of a 'big city' appeared, von Platen-Hallermund knew that he was not over the Humber, although he believed he was actually to the north of it. The lights of the 'big city' were in fact King's Lynn and within the crew's confused state they also believed they had received 'heavy artillery and infantry fire', which they attacked with high explosive and incendiary bombs. It can also been seen from von Platen-Hallermund's account that regardless of the inclement weather report, Zeppelin L-4's intended target was still to be Humberside.

Zeppelin L-4's Commander, von Platen-Hallermund and his crew were all decorated with the Iron Cross for undertaking the raid. Although, like her sister ship, Zeppelin L-4 and her crew did not have long to savour their accomplishment. On the 17th February, 1915, flying off the coast of Denmark, L-4 suffered a catastrophic loss of electrical power and lost use of its engines.

Von Platen-Hallermund managed to execute an emergency landing on the shore at Blåvandshuk, Denmark. Four crew were killed in the crash and the rest, including von Platen-Hallermund, interred for the rest of the war.

In the days following the raid, the sense of shock within the population of King's Lynn began to ease somewhat. A selection of bomb shells from the raid were put on public display at the Stone Hall, the admission charged for entry raisng £3 towards the victims of the raid. On a national level, the *Daily Mail* set up a £10,000 Zeppelin Fund for victims of Zeppelin raids, offering:

£200 - for each registered reader killed by aerial attack or
    bombardment from the sea or by anti-aircraft guns.

£200 - for the husband or wife or for each son or daughter of a
    registered reader killed through such causes.

£25 - for the death of each child below the age of 21.

£100 - for loss of one limb or one eye of an adult.

£2 - per week for a period not exceeding 15 weeks for total
    temporary disablement of any adult.

Up to £300 for damage to home furniture and personal effects.

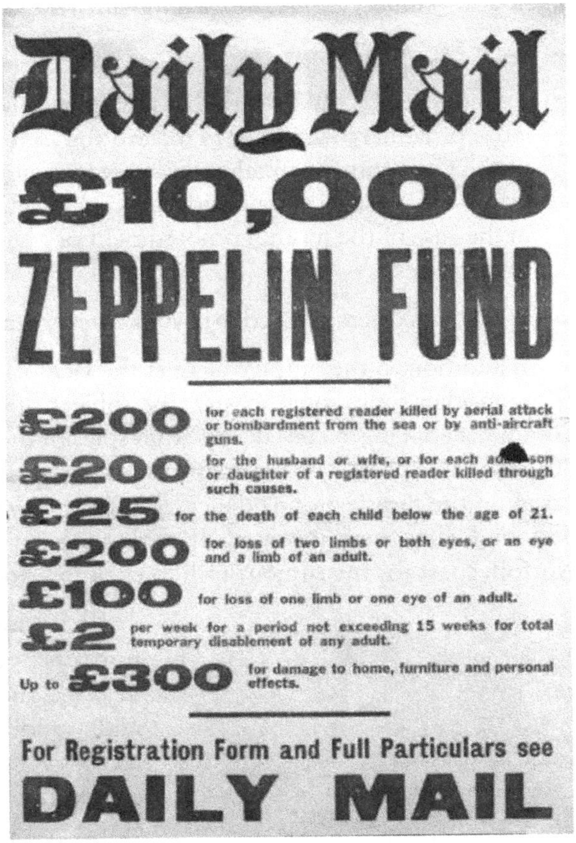

Once the shock of the raid had subsided, the general mood of the town turned to one of anger and much of this was directed at the government and War Office. The *Lynn News* ran an editorial decrying the lack of protection against the Zeppelin threat and offering its own independent solution 'Lynn Corporation, despairing of protection by the War Office and Admiralty, should itself purchase high angle guns and an aeroplane'.

On the 22nd January, 1915, the mayor of King's Lynn, Mr R.O. Ridley, wrote to the Prime Minister, Herbert Asquith, requesting that urgent consideration be given to compensating those who had suffered injury, damage or loss during the raid. The mayor also raised the question of what was being done to offer protection against further Zeppelin attacks.

Plate 2.18
A poster detailing the fund set up by the *Daily Mail* to help the victims of the Zeppelin raids.

Sir,

In reference to the raid of this town by the enemy's aircraft on Tuesday evening last, the 19th inst. I am directed to inform you that considerable damage was done to property of the very poorest classes. As a result various people are homeless and others are suffering greatly in consequence of the loss and damage to their furniture.

I shall be glad of an early intimation of the Government to compensate the people seriously affected. In the meantime, may I ask that some steps may be taken to relieve cases of immediate necessity?

I am to further call your attention to the fact that no protection of any kind is afforded to the town against raids of the above description and I beg to strongly urge that in view of the great probability of further occurrences of a like nature, some steps be devised to deal with them.

I believe I am fully alive to the difficulties of the situation and I know that great efforts are being made by His Majesty's Government in connection with the conduct of the war. I do suggest, however, that the matter referred to is of great importance and calls for some action to be taken.

The mayor's request drew a prompt response from Asquith and in a letter, dated 25th January 1915, the Prime Minister's office replied:

Dear Sir,

I am desired by the Prime Minister to acknowledge the receipt of your letter of January 22nd and to inform you in reply that it is the intention of the Government to take measures to deal with the damage suffered by reason of the recent air raids on King's Lynn similar to those adopted in the case of the recent bombardment of Hartlepool, Scarborough and other places.

The other matters referred to in your letter are receiving careful consideration.

In addition to the outrage against the lack of protection from the German raids, another topic soon became the subject of many conversations; had the German Zeppelins received help from spies in the locality? Since the outbreak of war, many people of German origin across Britain had become suspects based on the flimsiest of evidence, or often no evidence at all. If spies couldn't be found, they were invented. It took an event such as the raids along the Norfolk coast for the rumour mill to click into top gear.

Plate 2.19
Holcombe Ingleby (here dressed in less formal attire), who was M.P. for King's Lynn at the time of the raid.

The most widely spread of these rumours was that German spies were in place and active on the night of the raid; guiding the Zeppelins to their respective targets through a series of clandestine signals from car headlamps and then by using high powered torches to illuminate the targets themselves. Accounts passed by word of mouth that spies had been arrested and detained; some of these rumours found their way into the local press.

However, one local resident was to take a keen interest in these rumours and pursued them with furious vigour. Holcombe Ingleby was the MP for King's Lynn and lived at Sedgeford Hall, close to where some of Zeppelin L-4's earlier bombs had been dropped. A larger than life and very flamboyant character, he had toured the area by car on the morning following the raid. Stopping at Snettisham, he joined a group of villagers who were discussing the attack. The vicar, Rev. Charlton, asked Ingleby if the raid had been carried out by a Zeppelin or an aeroplane. One of the villagers was adamant that he had observed a biplane dropping the bomb on the church, exclaiming 'does a Zeppelin travel sideways?'

Meeting these villagers in the aftermath of the raid, such as at Snettisham, was where Ingleby first picked up the stories of German spies operating in the area. He first expressed his concerns about such suspicious activity on the night of the raid in a letter to *The Times* which was published on 22nd January, 1915:

> Your readers may like to receive from someone on the spot, an account of the Zeppelin raid to which we have just been subjected in this corner of Norfolk. The unwelcome intruder hovered round Hunstanton and the adjoining places for nearly an hour, apparently undetermined what course to take, or missing the objects of its intended attack. For obvious reasons I refrain from indicating these. It then dropped a bomb on the little watering place of Heacham. The bomb is stated to have fallen into a tub of water and to have destroyed the wall of a house without injuring its inmates. The airship then did me the honour of circling around my house, but happily, considering me unworthy of notice, it made off in the direction of Snettisham.

> I have myself tested the evidence of some of the most trustworthy of the inhabitants and the evidence seems to be worth recording. The Zeppelin is said to have been accompanied by two motor cars, one on the road to the right, the other on the road to the left. These cars occasionally sent upwards double flashes and on one occasion these flashes on the car on the right lit up the church, on which the Zeppelin attempted to drop a bomb. Fortunately the missile fell on the grass meadow separated from the church by the high road, but the force of the explosion was so great that most of the windows on the south and east sides of the church were blown in, together with some of the stonework of the mullions. Tablets in this part of the church were knocked down and other damage done. Snettisham church is a beautiful specimen of late 14th century architecture and it is fortunate that it escaped serious damage.

> After this attempt at wanton mischief, the Zeppelin made for King's Lynn and here again there is further evidence that it was accompanied by a car with powerful lights which at one time directed on the Grammar School. The car was stopped in the town and attention was called to the lights as a breach of regulations. Having put them out the driver turned the car quickly round and made off at rapid pace for the open country.

> Seven bombs were dropped on King's Lynn, two of them right in the heart of the crowded streets. Possibly they were intended for more

important buildings, which, without the aid of the car, it was difficult to distinguish. Two lives were lost and some 20 persons were injured, most of them not seriously. It is a miracle that the loss of life was not greater, seeing that four sets of premises were destroyed and several other houses more or less seriously damaged.

It was stated by two witnesses at Snettisham that they distinctly saw a biplane at the time the bomb was dropped and indeed, that they thought the biplane had dropped it. This statement, whether or not entitled to credence, tempts me in conclusion to draw attention to the fact that this part of the East Coast is, as regards aircraft, insufficiently guarded. A couple of biplanes at King's Lynn and a couple at Hunstanton might make such a raid as that to which we have been subjected impossible of success. If they could not destroy a Zeppelin, they might at least drive it off.

In the House of Commons on Tuesday 26th January, Sir William Bull asked the Prime Minister Herbert Asquith if he was aware of the allegation that the Zeppelin which had bombed King's Lynn had been guided by signals from two motor cars. Replying for the Prime Minister, Mr Reginald McKenna the Home Secretary said that the allegations had been carefully investigated by Norfolk constabulary. Eight cars had been traced as being on the roads during the raid and in each case their movements had been satisfactorily explained. All occupants were people of which there were no possible grounds for suspicion.

However, Ingleby refused to relinquish his pursuit on the possibility of German spying activity taking place within his constituency and with the febrile atmosphere of the time generating many letters describing similar strange events, Ingleby wrote a further letter to *The Times* on Thursday 28th January:

'I regret I was not in the House of Commons when the Home Secretary, in answer to a question put by Sir William Bull, unexpectedly made a statement regarding the motor cars alleged to have accompanied the Zeppelins in their raid on the East Coast. Perhaps under these circumstances, you will kindly allow me the hospitality of your column in order to submit a counter statement, for I am anxious that the public should be placed in possession of the real facts of the case.

Let me first test the value of the Home Secretary's statement that there were eight cars traced by the Norfolk Constabulary about the time of the raid and satisfactorily accounted for. The Constabulary were singularly blind that night. There were no less than six cars in different parts of Snettisham at the time mentioned, three of which were open to the gravest suspicion. Of these three the constable saw nothing. Similarly, the constable stationed at Heacham, where two bombs fell, informed me that after 6.30pm no car passed through that place. As a matter of fact two cars visited the lower part of the village, one immediately before and one immediately after the raid, and both excited suspicion. Again, within 20 minutes of each other three cars dashed through Brancaster Staithe, which is 10 miles distant from Heacham, the last one closely followed by the Zeppelin. The audacity of the occupants of that car passes belief, but in order that the statement of the witness I am about to quote may not be brushed aside too lightly, I ought to explain that the Zeppelin, whilst over Brancaster Staithe, was flying very low. scarcely higher, as another witness states, than the telegraph wires. And I may as well say here that all my statements are based upon the evidence of what I believe to be perfectly credible witnesses. Here is the statement referred to:

"On that particular night I was in my house at Brancaster Staithe. About 10.00pm I heard a Zeppelin passing over the house. It remained some minutes above the field adjoining, as if uncertain about something. A motor car with the most brilliant headlights imaginable then rushed along the road from Deepdale towards Brancaster, and when by the side of the field mentioned, above the occupants in the car all shouted very loudly, and two small lights were flashed from the Zeppelin as a reply. Then the latter travelled off after the motor car. I saw the headlights and heard the shouting but did not see the two lights from the Zeppelin, as I was in the front of the house; but the lights were seen by other occupants of the house … My observations were those of many people in Brancaster Staithe".

When it is remembered that the night was very still and that the Zeppelin (as remarked to me by witnesses in other parts of the county) occasionally shut off her engines, I submit there is nothing incredible in this statement.

I have a number of letters before me giving evidence of the presence of motor cars that night in various parts of the county, but it is unnecessary to labour that portion of the evidence. Correspondents from all part of the county speak of seeing a motor car with extraordinarily powerful lights in different places followed by an airship and sometimes throwing up flashes. A well known and much respected farmer living on the land high above Snettisham church speaks to seeing flashes of light sent up from six different parts of the neighbourhood. He has forwarded me a diagram giving the approximate position of the Zeppelin as judged by the noise of her engines, and the spots whence the flashes proceeded. Another farmer, also perfectly trustworthy, gives evidence of a powerful light on the other side of Snettisham being directed on the church a moment before the dropping of the bomb. There are eight credible witnesses who can speak to the flashes that proceeded from 'Sixpenny Hole' and attracted the Zeppelin to the church. The car that threw these flashes went off by a narrow side land, which no one who could avoid it would take by night. This car reappeared at the turning into Dersingham, and there threw up what appeared to be a definite signal - two upward flashes and one cross flash. At the turning by the church, which leads directly to Sandringham, it threw up more flashes. Similar evidence is forthcoming from other districts from west to east, right up to the suburbs of Norwich. What a strange series of coincidences are required to explain the circumstance that a powerfully lighted motor car constantly proceeded the Zeppelin in its journeyings through Norfolk that night! And can anyone suggest a reason why the sober inhabitants of Norfolk should be found rushing about the county at a particular moment bombarding the heavens with flashes?

Many of us have a great admiration for our Norfolk Constabulary, who are a fine set of men, and do their duty to the best of their ability. They are usually, however, planted at night in the main streets of our villages and there is no need for anyone bent on devilry to trespass on their beat. They saw nothing of motor cars on the night of the raid, and they are not willing to accept evidence that they cannot personally verify. I was afraid that the Under Secretary of State for War, relying on their evidence, might give a wrong answer to the question I put to him in the House on Monday last, that I called at the War Office on the previous Saturday and produced certain evidence for his guidance, if necessary. Indeed, a suggestion which I accepted, was made to me that an officer should call and examine the evidence in my possession. In the meanwhile the Home Secretary has rushed in with a statement which ought not to have been made until that evidence was tested. Had such been the case, I feel sure his answer to Sir William Bull's question would have been on entirely different lines.'

Holcombe Ingleby was not alone in raising questions about German spies operating in the area leading up to the raid. The *Lynn Advertiser* of Friday 22nd January carried several accounts of suspicious activity in the town preceding the Zeppelin's arrival. Mr C.M. Winlove Smith of Wootton Road, Gaywood told the paper:

'I had been home twenty minutes on Tuesday night when my wife noticed the windows being violently shaken, as though by a violent puff of wind.

Almost immediately afterwards came another gust and I went outside to see what was happening. There seemed to be nothing doing, but as I turned to go into the house I heard a sound that I knew well to be that of an aerial engine.

I immediately took precautions to put my wife and family in as safe a place as possible and went out into the garden, having extinguished all the lights.

The sound grew very much louder and I was soon able to determine by its sound that it was an airship and not an aeroplane. Later I was able to distinguish its outline and recognised it as a Zeppelin.

It was coming from the direction of Hillington and before it reached me I saw three flashes indicating that three time fuses had been ignited as bombs were dropped.

Just before the airship reached me a dark coloured, covered-in car passed along the road from the same direction. It had two enormous headlights, but no side or rear lights. It travelled very swiftly and silently into Gaywood, went a little way up the Gayton Road and stopped.

The airship came on and shortly after passing my house its engine stopped, giving the impression that the pilot had lost his bearings.

Directly after that the motor car came rushing from the Gayton Road and went swiftly towards King's Lynn. Instantly the engine of the airship was started again and I could see the machine making a circling movement.

When it got over what I took to be The Chase area the engine stopped again the airship appeared to circle back past my house and then go on again in the direction of the town.

Almost immediately after the first stoppage it commenced to drop bombs and from that time until it had completed its journey over the town I saw nine flashes indicating that number of bombs had been dropped.

Over by the Docks the airship appeared to wait again for guidance, for it hovered there quite five minutes and then crossed our house again and sailed off in the direction of Grimston.

As the airship came our way the motor car returned, still travelling at a tremendous pace and went in the direction of Knight's Hill.

A friend of mine saw what was evidently the same car standing in the High Street whilst bombs were actually being dropped in the town.

Another resident, a Mr W.F. Attwood of London Road, King's Lynn, also spoke of seeing a car that appeared to be communicating with the Zeppelin during the raid:

'I was in my house at about five minutes to eleven when I heard a noise which I took to be a traction engine passing. I went outside and that the noise came from above.

Looking up I saw a small green-bluish light going towards South Gates. It was evidently attached to the Zeppelin but I only saw the airship as something resembling a big black cloud; I could not distinguish its outline.

The noise and the light travelled southwards and I lost sight of the light for a time. Suddenly a motor car with four dazzling lights on the front of it came through the Gates and within minutes the Zeppelin came back. As the car passed All Saint's church room some soldiers came out and shouted "put your lights out".

The car ran rapidly along London Road and the Zeppelin followed. I saw a bomb dropped, apparently the one that fell in Bentinck Street, followed by another one close by. The car kept on its way and I did not see it again.'

Based purely on the fact that during this raid, Zeppelin L-4's commander and crew had no clear idea of their exact position, the suggestion that they were able to link up and communicate with pre-arranged spies on the ground is fanciful in the extreme. The occupants of the 'suspicious' cars seen were in all likelihood like many others that night, startled and intrigued observers, who as car owners had the ability to follow the action as it unfolded.

Following the raid on King's Lynn, new lighting enforcement regulations came into effect the following day:

Every streetlamp to be extinguished by 8 o'clock in the evening.

Householders are required to shade their windows so that no light can be seen from the outside.

Arrangements have been made with the police throughout the eastern counties to give early intimation of any future raid. On receipt of such warning, the electric current will be shut off and the public are required to extinguish all lights and fires. The Home Secretary has published in a notice prohibiting the use of powerful lights on motor or other vehicles.

In giving notice of the new lighting arrangements, notification was also given that the annual mart and fair which usually began on the 14th February would not be held that year. The Mayor issued the following message to go with the new regulations:

I take this opportunity of expressing the admiration I feel at the excellent conduct of the inhabitants during the recent raid and feel sure they will do their utmost to carry out the foregoing regulations.

R.O. Ridley, Mayor

Holcombe Ingleby's request for biplanes to be stationed at King's Lynn and Hunstanton was never implemented but it was not to be long before an airfield was established nearby to protect North West Norfolk from further Zeppelin attacks.

Chapter 3

The shooting down of Zeppelin L-70

Bank Holiday Monday on the 5th August, 1918 had been seen Great Yarmouth record its warmest temperatures for seven years. Crowds had thronged to the beaches throughout the day to enjoy the sun, sea and sand; attempting to seek respite from the Great War that still lurched on unmercifully but was starting to show the faintest signs of a conclusion. Those that decided to remain on the sea front into the late evening would have seen one of the most spectacular sites to occur over wartime Britain. The pride of the German Zeppelin fleet, L-70, was engulfed in flames, breaking into two and plunging into the sea off the north Norfolk coast. Afterwards, Kapitänleutnant Michael von Freudenreich, commander of the accompanying Zeppelin L-63, was to comment 'It fell like a huge sun. She went down like a burning arrow' Amongst Zeppelin L-70's crew of twenty two, was the chief commander of the German Imperial Navy Zeppelins, Fregattenkapitän Peter Strasser. The loss of L-70, along with the death of Strasser, was to mark the German's final air attack on England of World War One.

Zeppelin L-70 was one of the most technically advanced airship of the First World War. Its development began in December 1917, essentially as a result of the 'Silent Raid' on the Midlands and London of 19th October, 1917. While no airships were lost to British Home Defence forces on the raid itself, the eleven Zeppelins ran into a severe storm on the return journey. Unable to climb above the storm, gales scattered the fleet widely across Germany, the Netherlands, Belgium and France; five airships were lost with a total of twenty two crew killed and fifty two taken prisoner. Following an enquiry into this catastrophic loss, the German Admiralty pursued the development of larger

Plate 3.1

Fregattenkapitän Peter Strasser, chief commander of German Imperial Navy Zeppelins

airships which could climb to new altitudes and with much higher speed capabilities. By June 1918, four new airships would be ready, which in the words of Strasser would 'be capable of reaching the great altitudes over the

North Sea and England which are now required to carry out their missions, will at my insistence be high-climbing 7-engined ships of great speed'.

On Monday 1st July, 1918, Zeppelin L-70 left her hangar at Friedrichshafen for her maiden flight. Of a similar design to the earlier 'height climber' class, L-70 measured 693 feet 11 inches in length and had a gas capacity of 2,195,800 cubic feet. Powered by seven Maybach engine (one engine in the forward car, two in the rear gondola and two pairs affixed to two smaller gondolas amidships) L-70 reached trial heights of 19,700 feet and a maximum speed of 81 mph, making it the fastest airship built to date. It had the capacity to carry a 3,000 kg bomb load for raids on London and a powerful 4,700 kgs for lower level raids on the Midlands. Carrying a crew of twenty-two, the L-70 was also heavily armed to ward off any attacks by British aircraft; two Becker 20mm cannons mounted on the control car firing a combination of ball, tracer and explosive ammunition could easily pick off aircraft before they came into range. Strasser described the L-70 as the 'final type' and was eager to test its capabilities on England.

Plate 3.2
Zeppelin L-70 at its base at Friedrichshafen. Strasser believed its superior design to be the 'final type' and that it would go on to dominate the skies.

However, not everyone within the German Admiralty shared Strasser's confidence in L-70's prowess, particularly the airship's defensive capabilities. Admiral Starke, the head of the Aviation Department at the German Admiralty, later recalled a discussion where Strasser had tried to convince him that the danger of attack by aircraft to the L-70 was 'not great'. Strasser's hubristic declaration drew an unerringly prophetic response from Starke. 'Here I could not agree with him. I told him that I did not feel L-70's performance was sufficient protection against attacking aircraft'.

On Monday 5th August, the East Coast of England had not been the only location experiencing the warmth of summer. Northern Germany had also been basking in high summer and on the eve of a new moon, Strasser issued orders for a raid that he would command himself. Five Zeppelins – L-53, L-56, L-63, L-65 and L-70 – were to 'attack on the south or middle (London only at order of Leader of Airships)'. Weather conditions may have been ideal for sunbathing but with temperatures reaching 75° F and humidity reaching

85%, the extremely low barometric pressure was far from ideal to enable the airships to attain lift and the required altitude.

Notwithstanding that he held the rank of chief commander of the Imperial Navy, Strasser still made a habit of actively participating in raids upon England and on this day he would be travelling on L-70. The airship itself would be commanded by Kapitänleutnant Johann von Lossnitzer; a questionable choice given von Lossnitzer's limited combat experience, particularly over the North Sea. However, von Lossnitzer appears to have been a favourite of Strasser and was entrusted with the command of the most technically advanced airship of World War One, a craft that Strasser claimed could '...fly to New York, bomb the city and return to base without refuelling'.

The raid orders issued by Strasser on the morning of the 5th August were diligently outlined to the commanders of the Zeppelins taking part in the raid:

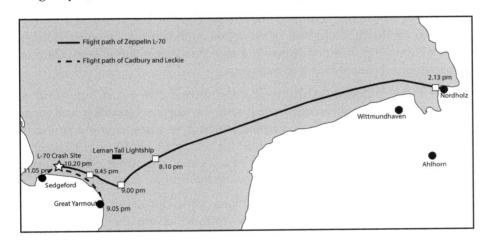

Fig. 3.1
The flightpath of Zeppelin L-70 on the night of 5th August, 1918

Attack in south or middle (London only at order of Leader of Airships). Bombs: Four of 300, four of 100, twelve of 50 kg. For L-70, eight of 300, eight of 100, eight of 50 kg. Takeoff for L-56, 3 p.m., the others at 2 p.m. Approach along the 54th parallel as far as 4 degrees east. Participants: L-53, L-56, L-63, L-65, L-70. Blankenberghe wind measurements at 2 p.m., 5 p.m., 5 a.m. Wind measurements from German Bight as required. Afternoon weather map will be wirelessed, night map will not. Preserve careful wireless discipline. Airship special wavelength. Leader of Airships aboard L-70. Direction from Nordholz on Leader of Airship's instructions.

The weather forecast had projected that cloud cover over central England would be spreading east, thus enabling concealment once the North Sea had been crossed. With pre-flight checks completed, the fleet of airships left their respective hangars. L-63 taking off from Ahlhorn at 1.47 p.m. L-53, L-70 and L-65 leaving from Nordholz at 1.55 p.m., 2.13 p.m. and 2.37 p.m. respectively. L-56 was the last to depart, taking off from Wittmundhaven at 3.12 p.m.

As the Zeppelins climbed into the afternoon sky, their crews busied themselves with their respective individual duties. Life on board an airship had always been harsh for crew members, devoid of most comforts. It was also fraught with risk. After recovering from the initial shock of the Zeppelin raids during the earlier stages of the war, Britain's Home Defence artillery and aircraft had slowly got their act together. German airships could no longer attack with impunity. A co-ordinated strategy of additional and heavier anti-aircraft weapons, combined with dedicated aircraft that were able to quickly reach the same heights as the Zeppelins, had caused the Germans to develop a new class of airship. During March of 1917 the first of the 'height climbers' launched their first raids over Britain. The Forties series of Zeppelins were now capable of reaching altitudes of 20,000 feet, the first time manned flight had reached such heights. While offering a respite from ground artillery and aerial attack, operating an airship at these heights brought a new set of problems.

The biting cold had always been a debilitating factor for airship crews operating in sub-zero temperatures. During the first years of the war, crews were required to wear service uniform with a greatcoat to ward off the cold. It had only been latterly that specialist fur-lined clothes, thick woollen gloves and felt overshoes had been issued. Newspapers were often stuffed between clothing layers to offer additional insulation. Food on board usually consisted of frozen sandwiches and bars of chocolate, with warmth being supplied by flasks of hot coffee. In some instances, Zeppelin commanders allowed the crew a strictly administered ration of Schnapps.

For some members of the L-70 crew warmth, of a sort, was possible. These were the machinists; involved with the ongoing servicing and repair of the airships engines. The powerful Maybach engines certainly emitted a considerable amount of heat within the confined working environment, however it unfortunately formed part of a cocktail of noxious exhaust fumes, this combined with the excruciating roar of the engines themselves.

However, freezing temperatures (along with the never distant fear of travelling aloft in a giant cigar-shaped cylinder of gas bubbles filled with highly flammable hydrogen) was not the only problem that the crew of L-70 would have had to contend with. The capability of attaining altitudes in excess of 20,000 feet also meant enduring the severe symptoms of altitude sickness. Today, through medical research, science is far more aware of the causes and the often dangerous effects of operating at high altitude but at the beginning of the 20th century these hazards were largely unknown. Once above an altitude of 8,000 feet, crew members could suffer acute headaches, nausea and shortness of breath. Reaching the new heights of around 20,000 feet would see the onset of a whole new range of problems, including unsteady gait, gradual loss of consciousness, lack of judgement and retinal haemorrhage. To counter these conditions compressed oxygen canisters were initially issued but many crew members refused to use them as they were often contaminated with glycerin that caused even greater illness. By the end of 1917, liquid air, devised and produced by the Draeger Company, was introduced which resolved the problem. Nonetheless operating at these heights was still far from easy. It is worth reflecting that during World War Two, most pilots used oxygen systems when operating above heights of 10,000 feet.

Having assembled together at 16,400 feet, the five airships headed across the North Sea and by 6.30 pm, in still clear skies, they were 60 miles off the East Anglian coast. On board L-70, Strasser was making the final adjustments for the forthcoming raid. Born in Hanover on the 1st April 1876, Peter Strasser had joined the German Imperial Navy at the age of 15. After serving on SMS *Stein* and SMS *Moltke* and then studying at the Naval Academy in

Kiel, his rise through the ranks was a swift one and by the age of nineteen he had been promoted to the rank of Leutnant zur See. After serving on board several other ships and becoming an accomplished gunnery officer, he was placed in charge of shipboard and coastal artillery in the German Imperial Naval Office. However, just prior to the outbreak of war, he was transferred to take command of the Naval Airship Division. At the time, Strasser considered this move to be a demotion but this opinion was soon to change.

Strasser was quickly able to grasp the potential of the airship, a still new and emerging technology, and the possibilities it held in writing a new chapter in modern aerial warfare. He was one of the first to conceive bombing attacks being used not just on military targets but also on civilians deep into the enemy's heartland. He was able to presciently foresee such raids as not just creating considerable propaganda value but also diverting valuable resources and material away from the enemy's front line. After the initial Zeppelin raids had been carried out over Britain, he was to famously declare 'We who strike the enemy where his heart beats have been slandered as baby killers … Nowadays, there is no such animal as a noncombatant. Modern warfare is total warfare'. In the world's first truly industrial war, there would be no safe havens behind military front lines. A threshold that would become truly obliterated to terrible effect just over twenty years later.

With dusk starting to approach, Strasser gave the order to descend and make a low level run inland, a route which would skirt Great Yarmouth along the way. Strasser believed that the cloud cover over central England would spread across to the east. However, in the clear skies the airships were spotted at 8.10pm by the Leman Tail lightship, located about 30 miles off the coast at Happisburgh, which raised the alarm. Flying without the added security of cloud cover would have given Strasser and his fellow officers some pause but not unduly so; they were still confident in their superior altitude as they headed slowly towards the coast.

Meanwhile down on the ground, the alert from the Leman Tail lightship had sparked the defences along the east coast into action and daylight warnings began to be sounded. The *Eastern Daily Press* subsequently reported 'There was no sign of alarm; just the anxiety to get to cover in the event of anything happening. The police and special constables took up their positions and all arrangements in case of emergency were made'.

At 9.00pm, Strasser sent a Morse code message to the fleet of airships 'to all airships, attack according to plan from Karl 727. Wind at 5,000 metres, west-south-west three doms (13½ mph). Leader of Airships'. As the message was being received by the crews of the other airships, messages of a different kind were hurriedly being delivered by orderlies from the Royal Naval Air Service station at Great Yarmouth (South Denes). This communication included a special message which was shown on the screen at the local cinema, urging all officers and men present in the audience to immediately return to the station.

In a hall in Wellington Pier, just across the road from the air station, a group of people were enjoying a much more relaxed and convivial evening than those in the airships poised off the coast. A charity concert was being held that evening and attending was the squadron commander of the nearby air station, Major Egbert Cadbury. Born in 1893 at Selly Oak, Birmingham and educated at Leighton Park School and Trinity College Cambridge, Cadbury was the youngest son of George Cadbury and heir to the family chocolate business. He initially joined the Royal Navy as an Able Seaman but in May 1915 he had been commissioned into the R.N.A.S. as a Flight Lieutenant and based at Great Yarmouth Air Station. The station was an an important part of the East Coast home defence network and Cadbury, along with the station's other pilots, had flown numerous sorties against other Zeppelin attacks.

Until the 5th August, Cadbury's most celebrated encounter with a Zeppelin had taken place on the night of the 27th/28th November 1916. Ten Zeppelins had left Germany, formed into two groups, one to attack the North of England and the other the industrial Midlands. After dropping her load of 16 bombs on West Hartlepool, damaging 40 houses, killing 4 people and injuring 34, Zeppelin L-34 had been shot down by 2nd Lieutenant Ian Pyott, a South African based with 36 Squadron out of Seaton Carew. Flying at 9,800 feet, Pyott followed the airship for 5 miles, firing 71 rounds until he noticed a bright patch appear on the airship which rapidly spread, engulfing the whole Zeppelin in flames. Diving rapidly to avoid the flames from the stricken airship, Pyott himself suffered considerable burns to his face as his aircraft passed close to the conflagration. Falling into the sea off West Hartlepool at 11.50 p.m, the flaming wreckage of L-34 was so intense that it was seen by a pilot flying over Melton Mowbray in Leicestershire.

Plate 3.3
Zeppelin L-21 in its hangar. The airship was to be later shot down off the east coast on 27th/28th November 1916, with the then Flight Lieutenant E. Cadbury, a participating pilot in the Zeppelin's loss.

Another of the participating airships on the raid was Zeppelin L-21. It had flown over Yorkshire until it reached Stoke-on-Trent, where it dropped 30 bombs. Heading back home in the early hours, the airship developed mechanical problems, losing one of her engines just outside Peterborough. It was eventually able to cross the East Coast near Lowestoft as dawn was breaking. By this time the naval air station at Great Yarmouth had been alerted and sent up three BE2c aircraft piloted by Flight Sub-Lieutenant. E. L. Pulling, Flight Sub-Lieutenant. G. Fane and Flight Lieutenant E. Cadbury.

Cadbury was to later give his account of the attack on Zeppelin L-21.

'We had been warned that the Zeppelin had dropped bombs in the Midlands and was making its way to the coast and I, along with two other pilots, immediately got into to the air to wait for it. I saw the Zeppelin approaching the coast and immediately chased after it. It was flying at about 5,000 feet when I first saw it and I immediately climbed to 8,000 feet.

I went after it. I approached from the stern about 3,000 feet below and fired four drums of explosive ammunition into its stern, which immediately started to light. At the same time one of the other pilots was flying over the Zeppelin and to his horror he saw a man in the machine-gun pit run to the other side and leap overboard.

Having seen the Zeppelin circle down to the sea in a blazing mess - a most horrible sight - I went back to Yarmouth. I could not say I felt very elated or pleased; somehow I was overawed at the spectacle of this Zeppelin and all the people aboard going down into the sea.'

It appears that Cadbury played the pivotal role in the downing of L-21, from which no survivors were recovered. However, for some reason the Navy gave the greater credit to Pulling, awarding him the D.S.O. and Cadbury and Fane D.S.C.s. If not having his full role recognised for the downing of L-21 irked Cadbury he did not show it, although when he was abruptly interrupted at the concert on the evening of 5th August 1918 with news of the arrival of Zeppelins off the coast, the thought must have crossed his mind that if the the opportunity to tackle another airship presented itself, this time the glory would be his.

Plate 3.4
R.N.A.S. Great Yarmouth
(South Denes)

Cadbury takes up the story of the evening.

'Mary was singing at a concert across the road in aid of some charity and singing very well too. I was enjoying the music, and war and rumours of war were very far from my thoughts.

A cousin of Mary's staying with us and I were enjoying a particularly fine piece of music when a cross-eyed R.A.F. orderly struck me with his converging vision. I guessed I was wanted and hastened to join him. I dashed along the front, and to my intense surprise, saw an airship in the dim distance, silhouetted against an extremely bright, clear, northerly, evening light. This was about 8.45pm.

I learnt from HQ that three Zeppelins were at a point about 50 miles north-east of here, well to seaward. Knowing that there was only one machine available that had the necessary speed and climb – its twin having already gone – I saw that a race was to the nimblest, to the pilot who could get to the waiting seat.

I roared down to the station in my ever-ready Ford, seized a scarf, goggles and helmet, tore off my streamline coat and semi-clothed, with a disreputable jacket under my arm, sprinted as hard as ever nature would let me, and took a running jump into the pilot's seat. I beat my strenuous competitor by one fifth of a second'.

The machine that Cadbury had succeeded in taking was an Airco DH4 (A8032). Powered by a 375 hp Rolls Royce Eagle engine, the DH4 had a maximum speed of 123 mph and could reach a ceiling of 22,000 feet. With its forward firing Vickers machine gun and Lewis gun for the rear observer/ gunner, the DH4 was a worthy adversary for any airship.

Plate 3.5
An Airco DH4 aircraft of the type used by Cadbury and Leckie in their attack on Zeppelin L-70.

Cadbury was joined in the DH4 by a Canadian, Lieutenant Robert Leckie, who was commander of the station's flying boat squadron (228). Although both Cadbury and Leckie were R.A.F. personnel, they continued to wear the uniform of the service that they had originally joined. Ironically, Leckie's combat achievements were linked to that of Cadbury's, having piloted the

Plate 3.6
Major Egbert Cadbury

H.12 flying boat that had shot down Zeppelin L-22 (the sister ship of L-21 which Cadbury had shot down) on 14th May, 1917. Like Cadbury, Leckie had not been expecting to fly that night and had no flying kit, not even gloves.

All told, the stations at Great Yarmouth, Burgh Castle and Covehithe were able to put thirteen aircraft in the air that night; a further DH4, five DH9s, five Sopwith Camels and one F2A flying boat. Aircraft were taking off as soon as crews were ready and the first to be in the air at 8.55pm was the other DH4, with Lieutenant R.E. Keys at the controls and Private A.T. Harman as observer/rear gunner. Cadbury was to follow shortly after at 9.05pm. Ten of the aircraft headed inland, while the remaining three, including Cadbury and Leckie, flew out to try and intercept over the sea.

As they climbed into the night sky, Leckie reflected on the uncharacteristic and brazen nature of the raid being undertaken by the exposed airships in such clear conditions. He was later to reflect 'I am still astounded at the audacity of the German commanders in bringing their ships so close to the coast of England in broad daylight'.

Taking almost an hour to climb up to 16,000 feet, Cadbury realised that the

Plate 3.7
Captain Robert Leckie.

aircraft was struggling and decided to jettison some of the smaller bombs it was carrying, along with the reserve fuel tank in order to lose weight. Finally breaking through the clouds, Cadbury could see three Zeppelins flying in a V formation to the north of Cromer, the airships silhouetted against the sky at around 17,550 feet. On seeing the approaching aircraft flares were dropped from one of the airships as they altered their course north. Off the coast from Wells-next-the-Sea, L-70 dropped three bombs which fell into the sea, close to the schooner *Amethyst*.

By 22.20, Cadbury had climbed to 16,400 feet and started to make preparations for his attack, selecting Zeppelin L-70 as his target. With L-70's immense shape hovering 2,000 feet above him, Cadbury brought his aircraft slightly to the port side of the Zeppelin, hoping to clear any obstruction that might be suspended below the airship. Closing to within 600 feet of her, he attacked head on. Leckie, hands numb with the bitter cold, aimed his Lewis gun at L-70's bow and fired a burst of tracer and incendiary rounds. The bullets found their target, tearing a large hole through the fabric at the base of the airship.

The Lewis gun's combination rounds accomplished their task, with the incendiary bullets quickly igniting the escaping gases. Cadbury and Leckie watched in awe as flames quickly ran along L-70's entire length. The stricken Zeppelin appeared to try and raise her bows in attempt to escape her death throes but silently she gave up the struggle. After a momentary pause, the airship plunged fully ablaze into the cold waters below. From the firing of Leckie's first shots, to being fully engulfed in flames, less than a minute had elapsed. As Cadbury and the other circling pilots watched L-70's fiery descent, a large petrol tank separated from the airship at around 7,000 feet. This was all that was seen to fall from the airship. No crew members were seen to leave the plummeting conflagration; either by choice or by force they remained onboard until L-70's charred frame crashed into the sea. The blaze from L-70 could be seen almost 40 miles away by the crew of the Leman Tail lightship and as far inland as Reedham. Having avoided L-70's falling bombs, the schooner *Amethyst* had a further fortunate escape when the flaming wreckage fell into the sea barely 300 yards away from it.

L-70's fiery descent was also seen by the crews of the remaining fleet. Kapitänleutnant Michael von Freudenreich, commander of L-63 recorded 'I

Fig. 3.2 Flightpath of Cadbury and Leckie and their engagement with Zeppelin L-70

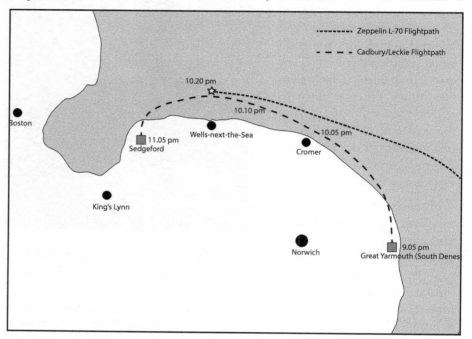

was nearing the coast when we suddenly saw an outbreak of flame on L-70 amidships or a little aft. Then the whole ship was on fire. One could see flames all over her. It looked like a huge sun. Then she stood up erect and went down like a burning shaft. The whole thing lasted thirty, maybe forty five seconds'.

Cadbury was to later recount his thoughts on the attack:

'It was a most fascinating sight - awe inspiring - to see this enormous Zeppelin blotting the whole sky above one. The tracers ignited the escaping gas, the flames spreading rapidly and turning the airship into a fireball in less than a minute. The L-70 dived headlong into the clouds. It was one of the most terrifying sights I have ever seen to see this huge machine hurtling down with all those crew on board'.

The new L-70 had not only been lauded for its attack potential but also for its defensive capabilities. Its powerful 20mm cannons were capable of ripping any aircraft to shreds. How were Cadbury and Leckie able to get such an unhindered attack on the airship?

Leckie was to later reflect on this:

'With reference to the attack upon L-70, I might say that the shooting from the Zeppelin was, as usual, very bad. This may be accounted for from the fact that the DH4 was practically invisible against the dark cloud beneath us. I would also point out that though I trained my gun upon the bows of the airship, fire was seen to concentrate well aft. I doubt very much if the German gunners allowed anything like enough deflection for their guns'.

Seeing the fate of their stricken colleagues, the two directly accompanying Zeppelins, L-53 and L-65, began to dump ballast, including a number of bombs, and turn for home. However, Cadbury had other ideas and he was soon putting his aircraft into a climb in pursuit of L-65, which commanded by Kapitanleutnant Walter Dose, had now climbed up to 19,400 feet. Leckie managed to fire off a few rounds at the fleeing airship and suddenly he saw a bright flash from the windows of the midships gondola. It was only after the war he realised that this light was not another fire but a member of the airship's crew inadvertently raising a blackout screen before the interior light was turned off.

As Cadbury's DH4 closed bow-on to the departing airship, L-65 opened fire with its Becker 20mm cannons, which proved wildly inaccurate against the advancing aircraft. With the DH4 now within 500 feet, Leckie took aim and pulled the trigger on his Lewis gun delivering a devastating burst; the rounds hit the midships gondola, causing a fire to break out. Preparing to fire another burst, Leckie's gun suddenly jammed. Without a coat or gloves in the frozen darkness, his numb fingers were unable to clear the clogged feed. 'Never in my life have I been so cold as I was that night, and the rear cockpit of the DH4 sure was draughty', he was later to recall.

Somehow the crew of L-65 managed to extinguish the fire within the gondola and after its struggle. was able to maintain its flight path. With Leckie's Lewis gun out of commission, Cadbury struggled to bring his Vickers machine gun to bear on the departing airship but the DH4 was reaching its ceiling. As he fought to bring the aircraft's nose up, Cadbury felt the aircraft suddenly stall and begin to fall back. Recovering from the stall, Cadbury managed to keep the aircraft in contact with the wounded airship for five minutes before he had to break off. Another aircraft tried to join the attack but was too low, leaving L-65 to escape for home.

Cadbury and Leckie were later to reflect on their aborted pursuit of Zeppelin L-65,

'Had we continued the chase to the end and destroyed the L-65 and L-53, we would have sacrificed the lives of another 150 to 160 very gallant men and not brought peace any nearer, because the loss of L-70 was a sufficiently severe shock to demonstrate the folly of sending Zeppelins near our coast'.

L-65 eventually managed to return to its base with some difficulty, as several of its gas cells had been holed.

There was however an even more important outcome of Cadbury and Leckie's curtailed pursuit; they had become lost in thick cloud. Not only lost but also flying an aircraft that didn't have the best of reputations for making night landings. The chances of making a return to Great Yarmouth, which had a very poor reputation for night landings at the best of times, were becoming more remote by the minute. The consequences of dumping their reserve fuel tank were now starting to bite. After flying through cloud for about 30 minutes, they suddenly spotted a burning flare path a few miles inland. The welcoming landing ground was R.A.F. Sedgeford, a Training School that also operated as a Night Landing Ground (NLG) for Great Yarmouth (other NLGs being at Narborough, Holt, Bacton, Burgh Castle, Covehithe and Aldeburgh). Alerted that aircraft were still up, Sedgeford had lit beacons on its landing ground and Cadbury managed to land safely and report in their victory. Although it was only after landing that he discovered why his aircraft had climbed so lethargically; the two bombs that he thought he had released were still primed and attached to the aircraft.

Not all the aircraft that went up to repulse the Zeppelin raid that night returned safely. A Sopwith Camel, (N6620), from Burgh Castle and piloted by Lieutenant G.F. Hodson was reported 'Killed In a Flying Accident'. A DH9 (D5802) from Great Yarmouth, piloted by Captain D.G.B. Jardine and his observer, Lieutenant E.R. Munday were reported 'Killed In Action'. Jardine had only arrived at Great Yarmouth that morning and he was on his first sortie. Bad weather may well have played a part in the loss of both aircraft. Some reports talk of one or both aircraft being confused by the flaming wreckage of L-70 floating on the sea. The debris burned for about an hour before it sank and the aircraft may have mistaken it as the flares from a Night Landing Ground before attempting to land on it. Jardine's body was subsequently washed ashore on the west coast of Jutland on the 26th September.

The remaining airships from Strasser's fleet made their separate ways back across the North Sea, although L-56 decided to head back down along the coast, arriving at Lowestoft just before midnight where she dropped three bombs at sea. The airship circled over the town before heading back out to sea, dropping a further fifteen bombs as it headed home.

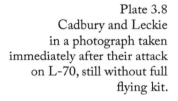

Plate 3.8
Cadbury and Leckie in a photograph taken immediately after their attack on L-70, still without full flying kit.

As they travelled over the sea's brooding waters, the fleet's crews would have been silently contemplating the fate of their departed comrades which they had recently witnessed. All Zeppelin crew members knew that the only certainty arising when an airship ignited was death. It was just a question of how; to jump or be burnt alive.

L-70 had crashed into eight fathoms of water, close to the Blakeney Overfalls bell buoy. The buoy was about eight miles north of Wells-next-the-Sea and almost fifty miles away from where Cadbury and Leckie had originally taken off from. In addition to seizing the prize of destroying another Zeppelin, it became immediately apparent to British Naval Intelligence that the crashed airship may also contain a bounty of vital information. Regardless of the fact that the remains of L-70 now lay in fifteen metres of very strong tidal currents, a plan was immediately put into to action to try and recover as much of the airship and all the documentary information it contained.

The first task was to locate the wreckage; this was undertaken by H.M. trawler *Scomber*. After the location had been marked with buoys, *Scomber* was joined by other trawlers; *Driver, Bullfrog, Peking, Topaz* and *Star of Britain*. The officer in charge of the operation was Lieutenant Commander J.H. Pitts. Using pairs of trawlers, cables were dragged under the water and between the 9th August and 22nd September, most of the wreckage was brought to the surface, where it was then transhipped to the port of Immingham. Cadbury was in fact invited to visit Immingham and select his souvenirs.

In addition to the wreckage of the downed Zeppelin, a vast quantity of documents were also recovered. These ranged from operating records to personal notebooks and journals. This not only provided British Naval Intelligence with the airship's design features and performance characteristics but quite possibly secret codes and ciphers as well.

The majority of the crew's bodies, including Strasser's, were recovered during the salvage operation. On his visit to Immingham, Cadbury recounts on being told that 'all the bodies were recovered intact, and that of Captain Strasser was completely untouched and his death was due either to drowning or to the shock of the impact with the water – I am not sure which – but he showed no disfigurement or burns or injuries of any kind'.

Strasser's body, along with a further five bodies that had been trapped in the wreckage of the airship when it smashed into the waves, were buried at sea. Other members of the crew had taken their chances by jumping to escape the flames. No parachutes were available for them to use. It was later reported that six or seven bodies were washed ashore along the Lincolnshire coast, prompting a hostile reaction from the local population when it was suggested that they be buried in a churchyard. Instead, the crew members were quietly taken out for burial at sea.

Of L-70's 21 crew members, just one was buried in England. A body was washed ashore on 6th October, 1918, about ten miles further down the coast from the airship's crash site. Buried in Weybourne cemetery, the grave is believed to be that of L-70's executive officer, Leutnant zur See, Kurt Krüger.

The body of L-70's commander, Kapitänleutnant von Lossnitzer, was among those recovered. A personal notebook was found on von Lossnitzer's body which contained invaluable information about L-70's performance characteristics. A dispatch case full of other documents was also recovered. As can be expected in such situations, British Naval Intelligence maintained a resolute silence on whether any codes or ciphers were obtained during the salvage operation.

After returning to his base at Great Yarmouth and catching up on some much needed sleep, Cadbury was to write reflectively on the previous night's events to his father: '... You will have heard probably before this reaches you

Plate 3.9
Blue plaque commemorating
Egbert Cadbury's residence
in Great Yarmouth.

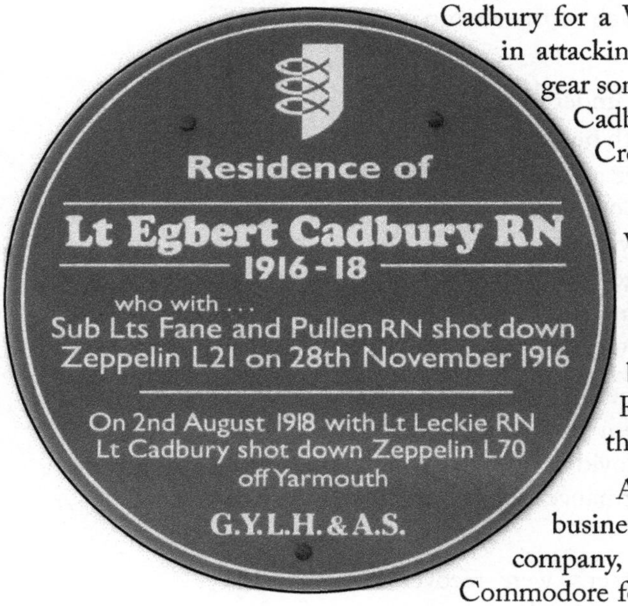

Residence of

Lt Egbert Cadbury RN
1916 - 18

who with . . .
Sub Lts Fane and Pullen RN shot down
Zeppelin L21 on 28th November 1916

On 2nd August 1918 with Lt Leckie RN
Lt Cadbury shot down Zeppelin L70
off Yarmouth

G.Y.L.H.& A.S.

that my lucky star has again been in the ascendant and that another Zeppelin has gone to destruction, sent there by a perfectly peaceful live-and-let-live citizen, who has no lust for blood or fearful war spirit in his veins'. For his feats on the night of the 5th August, the Commodore of Lowestoft recommended Cadbury for a Victoria Cross in recognition of 'his very great courage in attacking two airships with a land machine without floatation gear some 30-40 miles out to sea in bad weather'. However, both Cadbury and Leckie were awarded the Distinguished Flying Cross.

Unlike Strasser, both Cadbury and Leckie survived the war and were to go on and have divergent but equally successful careers. After WWI, Leckie was to direct flying operations for the Canadian Air Board. During WWII, he commanded British air forces in the Mediterranean before returning to Canada where he transferred to the Royal Canadian Air Force, becoming Chief of Staff and then a Canadian Air Marshal.

After the war, Cadbury was to join the family chocolate business, becoming managing director of his father's associate company, J.S. Fry and Sons Ltd. During WWII he was Air Commodore for the City of Bristol Squadron. Rejoining the Cadbury confectionery company after the war, he was knighted for his public services in 1957.

The downing of L-70 delivered a huge blow to the German Naval Airship Division but one which officials when to great lengths to conceal in their official statement, released in the aftermath of the raid:

'In the night of the 5th-6th August the so often successful leader of our airships, Fregattenkapitän Peter Strasser, attacked with one of our airship squadrons, again damaged severely the east coast of Middle England with effectual bomb attacks, especially on Boston, Norwich and the fortifications at the mouth of the Humber. He probably met a hero's death in the raid with the brave crew of his flagship. All other airships that took part in the attack returned without loss or damage in spite of strong opposition. Besides their experienced fallen leader, the airship commanders Korvettenkapitän J.R. Prölss, Kapitänleutnants Walther Zaeschmar, Michael von Freudenreich and Dose took part with their brave crews in the success.'

Behind the public praise and tribute to Strasser there was concealed anger and incomprehension of the risk he had taken in leading the raid in such vulnerable conditions. 'Whether in view of the cloudy weather, or trading on the immunity enjoyed in previous raids, Strasser showed remarkable recklessness in allowing his fleet to approach the English coast at a slow speed, at a comparatively early hour and a comparatively low altitude' thus concluded an anonymous German source. In later years, now Air Marshall, Leckie was to reflect that Strasser had been very unlucky with the weather but in final analysis still displayed poor judgement in proceeding with the raid.

'Following an almost perfect day with sky unusually clear of clouds, a heavy bank of nimbus spread from the West, and before the attack, had covered the East coast and sea to the east to 10/10ths. I feel it is more probable that Strasser was assured by his meteorological organisation that he could count on clear weather in the Bight of Heligoland and vicinity of the Dutch islands (making for easy and accurate navigation) and a thick cloud cover during the last 100-150 miles to his objective. We know the cloud cover did arrive but probably about 2 hours late. Unquestionably, however, Strasser exercised poor judgment in persisting with his operation without waiting for the cover of clouds'.

If the loss of the German flagship was not enough of a blow in itself, the tragedy of losing Strasser was even greater. The dynamic heart and soul behind the then new strategy of long-range bombing could not be replaced and his death was to bring to an end any further combat role for the Zeppelin. It was with some irony that the last attack by a German Zeppelin against the British Isles was to end not more than a few miles away from where the very first raid took place, that of Zeppelins L-3 and L-4 on the 19th January, 1915.

Chapter 4

Hippisley's Hut

By the outbreak of the First World War it had become evident that although still a fledgling technology, wireless communication was to be of vital strategic importance. A technology which would enable messages to be transmitted quickly over vast distances on land, sea and air. It was a young Italian, Guglielmo Marconi, who during the late 19th century had first considered and appreciated the commercial application of wireless telegraphy. Although his initial efforts transmitted signals just over one and half miles, Marconi quickly recognised the possible military applications of the technology. Marconi took his signalling system to the Italian government who showed no interest in it whatsoever.

Undeterred, Marconi moved to England in February 1896 where he registered a patent for his wireless system and in August of the same year he had demonstrated his wireless equipment at a conference at the War Office. The Royal Navy were impressed enough to mention Marconi's promising experiments with 'electric signalling' in its Annual Report of the Torpedo School, highlighting the potential for torpedo boats to indicate their approach or proximity to friendly ships.

Plate 4.1
Guglielmo Marconi, developer of the first effective system of radio communication.

By 1899 wireless sets were being used, with varying degrees of success, by British forces during the Boer War. Other countries soon adopted wireless military communication but what was evident from the outset was that this new technology had one serious weakness. Highlighted by the Russian-Japanese war in 1904, both sides were able to listen in to each other's communications. It was not possible to hide the signals. Another aspect of wireless communication was soon recognised in that it was also possible to locate their source of transmission. Even at the outbreak of hostilities during the First World War, Russian messages were still being sent uncoded and as such intercepted by the Germans. The Russian author Alexander Solzhenitsyn was to later note that the Russian Imperial Command relied on transmitting their messages late at night in the belief that the Germans had gone to bed and weren't listening.

Plate 4.2
An example of a Marconi
wireless set.

Although the British had gained a significant lead in developing and applying Marconi's wireless communication, it was inadvertently relinquished when an in-depth article, outlining all the technical specifications, was published in a specialist publication. Germany was only too grateful to take advantage of this generosity and made huge strides with their own developmental plan. Both countries continued experimenting, trying to apply the technology to land, sea and air. The tandem development of military aviation offered significant potential but was limited by the size and weight of the wireless equipment used and having to transmit morse code messages while still attempting to fly the aircraft.

By 1908 the Royal Navy had implemented a small network of stations, including one in Gibraltar, that allowed communication within this network but importantly it also enabled the stations to convey basic command and control messages to the Royal Navy fleet in home waters. The stations were linked to the Admiralty at Whitehall. The outbreak of hostilities in August 1914, saw the British government take control of the existing Marconi and General Post Office stations. Like many technologies during the First World War, wireless communication would develop rapidly and deliver strategic information undreamt of in previous conflicts. Not only could wireless stations send messages over wide distances without having to rely on a cable network, thanks to the earlier work of Marconi they were also able to use detection finding techniques to locate from where a message was being transmitted. By intercepting enemy messages and triangulating their origin, it was possible to obtain accurate positions of enemy transmitters.

In 1907 the Post Office had built two such wireless stations on opposite sides of the Wash, one at Skegness and one at Hunstanton. Both stations were of identical layout, with the focal point being a 122ft high mast. They were operated on six hour shifts by a three man team, each of whom had been trained at the Torpedo School and were drafted into the Coast Guard Service.

Plate 4.3
Pre-1905 postcard showing
the clifftop lighthouse at
Hunstanton

Plate 4.4
1905 postcard showing
the clifftop lighthouse at
Hunstanton

Plate 4.5
Postcard showing the first
mast present on the site,
c.1907.

Plate 4.6
Postcard showing mast and
timber hut, adjacent to the
newly built Coast Guard
watchtower, c.1907.

At the outbreak of the war wireless sets were also being used by many
amateurs and despite the British government having decreed it illegal to possess
a privately owned set, two disparate enthusiasts continued with their listening
activities and through their joint work came into contact with one another.
Edward Russell Clarke, a barrister practicing in Abergavenny, had become
interested in this new technology and had begun isolating signals transmitted
from overseas stations. The other enthusiast in question was Richard John
Baynton Hippisley. Born on 4th July 1865 and educated at Rugby and later
Faraday House, London (the Electrical Standardising, Testing and Training
Institution) where he studied engineering and mathematics.

At the age of nineteen, Hippisley had inherited the family's Ston Easton
estate in Somerset. He had also inherited his grandfather's (who was a

Plate 4.7
Richard John Bayntun
Hippisley, an amateur radio
enthusiast who developed
the wireless listening station
at Hunstanton, which was
to become the birthplace of
wireless interception.

member of many of Europe's leading scientific societies) interest in science. After serving an apprenticeship at Thorn Engineering, he joined the North Somerset Yeomanry, becoming an Honorary Lieutenant Colonel in 1908. Hippisley maintained his interest in electrical engineering and by 1912 he was working in wireless telegraphy at a station at the Lizard in Cornwall. It would while working at this station that he picked up messages transmitted from the sinking Titanic. In 1913 he was appointed as a member of the War Office Committee on Wireless Telegraphy.

During the early months of the war, both Hippisley and Clarke had been receiving a large and regular number of messages which they believed to be originating from the German Naval wireless stations at Neumunster and Norddeich. The messages (often sent by and to the German fleet) the pair were receiving were being transmitted on a lower wavelength and as such were not being picked up by the existing network of Marconi stations.

After discussing the matter, the pair approached the Admiralty with the suggestion of setting up their own listening station. Lacking the resources themselves, the Admiralty were happy for them and many other enthusiasts to become Naval Voluntary Interceptors. In late 1914, Hippisley and Clarke were sent to Hunstanton to set up a wireless listening post. Hunstanton was ideally suited, being the highest point towards the German mainland, as well as being the existing home of the earlier wireless station. By this time Hippisley had become a Commander in the Royal Naval Reserve for service with Naval Intelligence.

Hippisley and Clarke had been recruited by Sir Alfred Ewing, who had been tasked by Churchill to set up a codebreaking team at the Admiralty. This small group would be based in Room 40 of the Admiralty Ripley Building in Whitehall. Room 40 would become the first home of British cryptography, opening in October 1914 and closing in February 1919. Up to this point Britain had no formal codebreaking operation. Under the mounting number of encrypted messages that were being intercepted, a trawl of naval colleges and universities was undertaken to enlist suitable recruits to undertake the decryption work.

Wireless stations such as that at Hunstanton (although Hunstanton was to quickly become known as Hippisley's Hut) performed several different roles:

Y stations were for the interception of wireless communications.

B stations were tasked with direction finding (D/F). Some stations, like Hunstanton, were designated both Y and B stations.

Ship to shore stations offered a two way communication facility.

Experimental stations carried out research and developmental functions.

Training schools for teaching new operators.

Imperial Wireless Chain stations which specifically linked countries within the British Empire.

General Post Office stations.

Many of the sites were located around the coast and usually an elevated point in the landscape was chosen, giving unimpeded transmission. Wooded areas were to be avoided, as these tended to distort nighttime signals. It was also found that sandy conditions close to coastal sites gave improved earthing. Many stations were positioned adjacent to lighthouses, allowing facilities and infrastructures to be shared. Additionally, proximity to an existing telephone line was also a factor. Inland located sites typically had an administrative or training role.

The key role of interception sites was to gather radio traffic which was passed directly to Room 40 at Whitehall, although some analysis did take place at a local level. Direction finding stations were tasked with trying to locate the point of origin of the transmission by by triangulating the source signal. Sometimes a station would combine both functions, although because of interference the direct finding operation was usually located away from the intercept operation in order to reduce interference. Hunstanton was also the temporary home for a direction finding station.

As the war developed, one particular area where wireless intercept stations were to prove invaluable was in the monitoring of Zeppelin activity. German launch procedures for Zeppelin raids usually followed a very rigid template. The first sign of launch preparation was the transmission of specific weather forecast information. Once airborne, Zeppelins would relay a confirmation back to their base and to assist with their navigation, airship crews would signal German wireless stations to confirm their location. All of this wireless activity could be intercepted by stations such as Hunstanton, who would then immediately convey it back to the Admiralty at Whitehall. Because Britain had a much more extensive network of wireless stations than Germany, the Admiralty was able to plot the Zeppelin locations to a far greater accuracy than the crews themselves.

At Hunstanton, Hippisley and Clarke were given a relatively free hand in conducting their operation and they soon became involved in establishing similar stations elsewhere. Upon arriving at the clifftop site, they found a wooden hut but no aerial! However, it did not take long for them to start collecting signal traffic. Soon the station at Hunstanton had grown large enough for the staff at Hunstanton to put together their own football team. As the station expanded, Hippisley was joined by another fellow alumnus from Rugby, Leslie Harrison Lambert. Lambert was a keen amateur wireless enthusiast who worked for the Foreign Office and would later become the well known BBC radio broadcaster, A.J. Alan, throughout the 1920s and 30s.

The station at Hunstanton soon acquired the name of 'Hippisley's Hut' and the work carried out there saw Hippisley given free rein to set up additional listening stations across the British Isles and also in Malta and Italy.

The work carried out at the wireless station at Hunstanton, along with others within the network, proved invaluable to the British war effort. By 1916, Hippisley's Hut was able to capture the orders given by Zeppelins as they left their sheds at their home bases, thus enabling Room 40 at Whitehall to give advance warnings of impending raids. Perhaps the most notable nugget of information intercepted by the Hunstanton wireless station occurred on 30th May, 1916. Hunstanton reported unusual amounts of message traffic

being produced by German warships from their port at Wilhelmshaven. By monitoring the bearing of the traffic, teams at the Admiralty were able to speculate that the German fleet were planning to put to sea. The British fleet were immediately informed and headed towards the German Bight, where the following day one of the most important naval battles of the war was fought – the Battle of Jutland. By intercepting the German communications, the British fleet were able to gain a four and half hours start before the German fleet had left port. Even though the British were to lose more ships during the battle, the German fleet was effectively taken out of operation and never put to sea again in any operational strength.

For his work on wireless interception during the war, Hippisley was awarded the O.B.E. On his death on 27th March 1956, his obituary in the Times described Hippisley as 'an almost unique personality' who 'inherited a remarkable mechanical and scientific gift, which put him in the forefront, if not ahead, of most of his contemporaries'. An associate recalled meeting an admiral after the Armistice who remarked that Hippisley 'was one of the men who really won the war'.

The typology of wireless station sites hanged significantly from their introduction and development throughout the war years. The first sites tended to be built in the main to independent designs and layouts, suiting their location and role. This also included the adaption of existing buildings on the sites. A typical site would have been enclosed and comprised of two to three wooden buildings (operations and accommodation), along with a tower and mast. Some sites, such as Poldhu in Cornwall, were quite large; the Poldhu site having six buildings, eight posts and five masts. Many of the buildings constructed were timber-framed, with weatherboarding on external walls and felt-clad roofs. Some stations, such as at Cullercoats which was built pre-war, were constructed with more robust materials comprising of brickwork walls and a slate tiled roof. Each of these different building designs has left a significantly contrasting archaeological footprint.

After the declaration of war, the War Office took over the construction of new wireless stations, in the process developing them to a standardised design. Records of building plans at two different sites, Lowestoft and York, show the different types of buildings used:

Lowestoft

Station A1 – two wooden buildings (26 feet by 12 feet) with 5 windows and shutters, and 5 masts

Station A2 – a wooden building (14 feet by 10 feet) with 3 windows and shutters, and 1 mast

Station F1 – two wooden buildings (54 feet by 12 feet) with 3 windows and 3 shutters and 5 x 180 feet box masts

Station F2 – 90 feet by 12 feet wooden cabin with 3 windows and shutters, and a 90ft mast

Station – same accommodation as F1

Engine house – wooden building measuring 11 feet by 7 feet, with 2 windows and shutters

A battery house – a portable wooden building (8 feet by 6 feet)

A guard room – a wooden building (10 feet by 12 feet, with 4 windows and 4 shutters and 10 wooden bunks)

2 canvas tents

2 dug-outs

4 sentry boxes

2 latrines

York

A cabin – used as a landline and 'AD' station (27 feet by 13 feet), which is weather boarded with 3 double and 3 single windows. Cabin divided into 2 rooms with 1 cooking stove and 1 open heating stove

Cabin – used for F1 and B1 station (15 feet by 10 feet) with 2 double and 1 single window. It was open plan with a heating stove

Weather boarded cabin – used for CD and J1 station (21 feet by 13 feet) with 3 double windows. Divided into 2 rooms with an open heating stove

Cabin – used for BD station (12 feet by 11 feet) with a heating stove

Guard hut (21 feet by 13 feet)

Engine house (11 feet by 7 feet)

Small hut – used as a battery house

Cabin on 4 small wheels, originally used as a builders' office

4 wooden sanitary huts

2 old canvas huts

1 corrugated iron lavatory

Most sites were enclosed with timber fencing or barbed wire for security reasons, several stations had their own guard detachment on site. The British government appears to have been relatively relaxed about the sites becoming public knowledge but went to extreme lengths to disguise the value of the information that was being intercepted and the methodology used to obtain it.

The most important building on the site was the wireless room. The room needed to be kept dry but also well ventilated, allowing the equipment to function, requiring it to have opening windows and louvre ventilations fitted into the roof.

The accommodation area and facilities were functional and basic, with some staff living off-site in local lodgings. Sleeping rooms usually had around six bunk beds and a wash basin. The mess room would have featured a larder, cooking range and table. The officer in command of the site would having his own room.

Most wireless stations were unmistakeable due to their masts and supporting cables. The masts varied in height and numbers from station to station. The Poldhu station had an array of masts, configured in a square formation, whereas others only had a single mast. An article in *Electrical Engineering*, dated 14th February 1907, describes the masts at Hunstanton and Skegness as of being of very noteworthy construction:

'Each has been built (in a horizontal position) out of deal planks treated with carbolinium. A start was made by placing together five planks of lengths varying from 5 to 25 feet; to this stump other 25 feet planks were laid on continuation, and the process continued, with proper tapering, till the whole mast length is formed without two butt joints ever coming together. The whole is bolted up by bolts every 18 inches. The lower part of the mast is eased around with four planks, but the upper part is planked only where the edges show. The masts being only one foot square at the base, prove very pliable in high winds, yet exceedingly strong. Each mast is stepped in concrete, and has three sets of four stays, which are tied to ground anchors consisting of long bolts through six foot oak baulks buried to a depth of six feet. The air-wire system consists of six equal wires hanging from a yard and spreader of oak. The wires at both stations dip at about 30 degrees from the vertical towards the north-east, and are held apart by insulated stays near the bottom. Here they are gathered into two bunches of three, and both bunches are insulated and led through an ebonite tube into the apparatus room.'

The article goes on to describe the engine and alternator being housed in a wooden outhouse, with dimensions of 12 feet by 8 feet. The Hunstanton site's telegraphic apparatus at the time the article was published, were housed in the newly built watch-room of the Coast Guard lookout tower. The window on the eastern side of the building, through which the leading-in wires from the mast fed into the watch-room is still identifiable today.

Wireless technology developed enormously, driven as it was by wartime necessity. The type of equipment used was dependent on the station type – naval, army, air force or land-based wireless station. During the early stages of the war, standard equipment comprised a spark transmitter, crystal receiver and a magnetic detector. By the close of the war, radio valve systems were being widely used.

It has proved difficult to discern the overall layout of the Hunstanton wireless station, minimal records exist and perhaps the best picture is obtained from a series of postcards which depict the sites development during the early part of the 20th century. The first postcard, facing east, depicts the lighthouse tower without its later extension and on the land in front of and to the east of the lighthouse and its associated buildings; a mast with tethering cables can be clearly observed. The mast is roughly parallel in height to the lighthouse tower, which at this time was approximately 50 feet (15m) in height. Wooden buildings related to the wireless station are not visible in the postcards. Also not visible in the image is the Coast Guard lookout tower, recorded as also being built in 1907. Part of the coastguard tower building was initially used to house the Post Office wireless station.

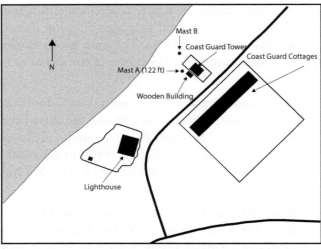

Fig. 4.1
Plan of the Hunstanton wireless station site.

Later postcards (identified as being the signalling or Marconi station) show the wireless station site being developed. The mast shown on the earlier postcards is still in place but it has now been joined by a second, much taller mast (122 feet). Some postcards show the mast standing without any cables, later ones show multiple cables tethering it to the ground. The later postcards also show a timber building located directly adjacent to the west of the Coast Guard lookout tower. It is likely that this building was the one that is now in use as holiday chalets in Old Hunstanton.

In *A History of Hunstanton* published in 1984, local author L.L. Gore suggests multiple locations for the siting of wireless stations, including the lighthouse building, an installation at Downes Road, a wooden clubhouse at the golf links and a wooden bungalow adjacent to the Cromer Road (it is possible that this latter location could refer to the wooden building at Holme-next-the Sea mentioned below). Although it has not been possible to authenticate the station's complete layout, it is certainly suggestive that not all functions of the wireless station were located on the clifftop site. The direction finding operation would have been placed some distance away and would almost certainly have been located at one of the sites mentioned above.

Plate 4.10
The site today, looking west. The area in front of the coastguard watchtower building would have been where the main mast would have been sited.

Plate 4.11
The site today, looking east. The timber framed huts used during the wireless statio's operational period would have been located on the grass area, adjacent the Coast Guard watchtower building, along with the earlier, smaller mast.

Today little evidence of the wireless station remains on the original clifftop site. During particularly dry summers, a cropmark is visible on the grassed area between the old lighthouse and coastguard tower. The cropmark appears to be the outline of a building, aligned east-west, measuring approximately 18 feet wide and 28 feet in length. This appears to be one of at least three single storey wooden buildings that comprised the site during the First World War. However, while evidence of the buildings does not remain on the original site, the buildings themselves have not moved very far over the years. Two of the wooden huts that were used at the station can now be found at a secluded holiday chalet in Old Hunstanton. It is not known when the huts were removed from the original site and placed either side of the main house and form a picturesque cottage.

Plate 4.12
The Hippisely Hut holiday cottage in Old Hunstanton. The original timber buildings from the wireless station are located either side of the main cottage.

It has not been possible to closely examine the buildings at Old Hunstanton to ascertain whether the two buildings were originally individual or if they have been separated into two upon relocation. The 'hut' on the right-hand side of the house measures 20 feet by 17 feet, the left-hand side 'hut' measuring 12 feet by 8 feet (matching the dimensions of the engine and alternator building referred to in the *Electrical Engineering* article). Both buildings are single-storey and are today positioned either side of a later, larger building. Each has been renovated, although they still retain much of their primary character. It appears that larger windows on the front elevation may have replaced the originals. In addition the building located to the left has had a new door added. Both buildings have pitched roofs.

A further timber building can be found at Holme-next-the-Sea, the next village along the coast to Hunstanton, where another of the huts from the station has been developed into a residential bungalow. For many years the building was home to Mrs Jean Tipple, who was actually born there in 1925. At this time the building had already moved from its clifftop location at Hunstanton and in 1927 it was moved again to its present site at Holme-next-the-Sea. The hut has been incorporated and developed into a residential building. It measures approximately 18 feet by 10 feet and is aligned north-south on the western side of the main building. The building has a window on its north elevation; it has not proved possible to ascertain if this was present in the original. The original weatherboarding remains in place, although the original felt roof appears to have been replaced with ribbed concrete tiles. The building rests on a brick foundation.

Plate 4.13
Northern elevation of 42 Main Road, Holme-next-the-Sea. This timber framed building was originally used at the wireless station at Hunstanton.

Plate 4.14
Western elevation of 42 Main Road, Holme-next-the-Sea.

Chapter 5

The History of Sedgeford Aerodrome in WWI

Just before 10.35 am on Friday 17th December, 1903 at Kill Devil Hills, a small town just outside of Kitty Hawk, North Carolina, two American brothers who ran a printers and a bicycle shop, Wilbur and Orville Wright, were preparing to make history. For three consecutive days they had taken their fledgling aircraft, *The Flyer*, to the same hill, specifically chosen because of its good winds. On the 14th December, after winning a coin toss to decide who would fly it, Wilbur managed to get off of the ground for just three seconds before crashing. On the 17th December, it would be Orville's turn and for twelve seconds he flew 120 feet in distance. In little over ten years after writing this first chapter of sustained flight, aircraft would be involved in one of the worst military conflicts that mankind had known.

Plate 5.1
The Wright Brothers achieving the first sustained flight of a powered aircraft with *Flyer 1* at Kill Devil Hills, North Carolina on 17th December, 1903.

Although aviation was to develop rapidly, the concept of using aircraft for a military role was not one that was immediately embraced by the British military forces. In 1911, Prime Minister Herbert Asquith had initiated a study to look at how aircraft could be used effectively and efficiently by the British military. The committee tasked with developing a proposal recommended the creation of the Royal Flying Corps (R.F.C.), which would comprise a military wing, a naval wing, a Royal Aircraft Factory and a Central Flying School. The

Royal Flying Corps was formed in April 1912, however, it was not too long before inter-service tensions raised their head. The Navy soon began to train its own pilots and by 1st July 1914 it had become completely independent, forming the Royal Naval Air Service (R.N.A.S.).

Plate 5.2
'The first machine to fly past on parade.' Major E.L. Gerrard, piloting a Henri Farman biplane, flying past General Sir H.L. Smith-Dorrien, at the Review held on Perham Down on Thursday 22nd May, 1913.

By the outbreak of war, roles for the respective services had been demarcated. While four R.F.C. squadrons had been sent over to France and the others undertaking the training of pilots back home, the R.N.A.S. had been tasked with defending Britain from aerial attack. Foremost within this threat to British shores was the menace of Zeppelins. A chain of coastal air stations was set up along the entire east coast of Britain. Due to the limited amount of time the aircraft were able to stay in the air, these bases had to be placed close to potential enemy interception points. Many of these Home Defence (HD) stations also had their own group of Night Landing Grounds (N.L.G.s), which enabled aircraft to use them in the event that they found themselves without enough fuel to return to their main station.

Fig. 5.1
Location map of Sedgeford aerodrome.

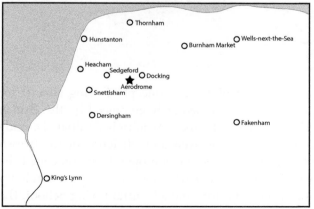

The Zeppelin raids carried out along the East Coast of England on the 19th/20th January, 1915 exposed the frailty of the British defences against aerial attack. The public outcry following the raids in Norfolk was soon to be followed elsewhere, as by the middle of June of that year there had been a further twelve Zeppelin raids undertaken on British soil. Targets all down the east coast, including London itself, had been hit; killing 58 people, injuring 165 and causing thousands of pounds worth of damage. But perhaps the most notable outcome of these attacks was the sense of fear that they instilled in the British public. Engendering terror had been one of the primary aims of the German Naval staff when they first formulated their plans for the Zeppelin raids against mainland Britain; cause panic within the population which in turn will exert pressure on the British government to end the war.

To assuage public opinion that the government was putting up a robust defence against the raids (or at least demonstrating that one was being prosecuted), the ribbon of air stations and night landing grounds around the coastline was quickly established. One of the night landing grounds was to be built on a ridge of Norfolk farmland overlooking the Heacham River valley, just outside of the small village of Sedgeford.

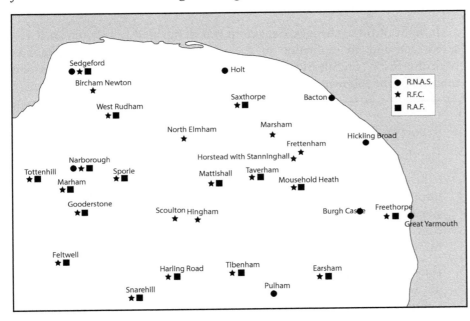

Fig. 5.2
Location map of Norfolk airfields in the First World War.

R.N.A.S. Landing Ground

The R.N.A.S. Landing Ground at Sedgeford came into operation during August, 1915. It is not known for certain if this was as a direct consequence of the raids by Zeppelins L-3 and L-4 during January of the same year and the vocal pressure that arose in its aftermath. Certainly, the area of the North Sea just off from the Wash was developing into an important nodal point for German flightpaths. Compared to what was to arrive later on at the site, the Naval presence at Sedgeford was a relatively modest affair. The landing ground was reached by a trackway that lead off from the Sedgeford to Docking road, with the modest R.N.A.S. quarters and hangar located directly to the south of a small area of woodland, known as Whin Close. The woodland was originally part of a small park that belonged to the nearby East Hall manor.

As a satellite for the main station at R.N.A.S. Great Yarmouth (South Denes), the landing ground at Sedgeford did not see a huge amount of activity during its early months of operation. The field was mostly used by aircraft from R.N.A.S. Great Yarmouth to make night landings after undertaking patrols. Occasionally it would receive their aircraft when they were dispersed prior to a Zeppelin raid to allow wider coverage. The landing ground did from time have its own aircraft stationed there, a BE2c night fighter. The officer in charge of the detachment at Sedgeford as Lt. H.C. Mallet RN and the pilot based here was Flight Lt. J.H. Lee.

During the early Spring of 1916 plans were at an advanced stage to change the roles within Britain's home defence system. The demarcation of responsibilities between the R.N.A.S. and the R.F.C. at the outset of the war had been reviewed in light of the R.F.C's subsequent development. On 10th February 1916, after much passionate debate within the British Cabinet, a new Home Defence plan was approved. The R.N.A.S. would be responsible for attempting to stop German aircraft from reaching Britain. The R.F.C. would take on the inland defence role, becoming responsible for dealing with any aircraft that made it through.

In light of these changes, Sedgeford was designated to become an R.F.C. aerodrome and an evaluation of the site was undertaken by Captain G. Malcolm R.F.C. on 5th March, 1916 prior to it moving under the control of the R.F.C. The following is Malcolm's report

---

Report on R.N.A.S. Landing Ground at Sedgeford

The shape is roughly rectangular.

I do not know the exact acreage. The R.N.A.S. Officer in charge is informing me of that tomorrow but it is well over 80 acres. The ground slopes steeply down in a south westerly direction from the south west edge. This slope is ploughed. There is no hedge or ditch separating this from the aerodrome.

The surface for the most part is good rough turf. Several potholes in the north western corner have been filled in and I am informed that there is a contract out for sowing these patches.

The surrounding country is very good except for several large woods. There is a wood on the north west edge of the ground.

This ground is suitable for a night landing ground. The soil is clay.

There is one aeroplane shed, without floor, measuring 66' by 52'. There is one Bessoneau shed which at present has no cover and is under repair.

The accommodation for the men is one hut of the same pattern as at Narborough viz. hammocks for seventeen men and two rooms - three beds for officers. There are five small - about 8' by 6' store huts and one petrol store, also a latrine.

Telephone – There is a direct line to the R.N.A.S. switchboard at King's Lynn – No. 220 King's Lynn. There is also an extension to the Coast Guard at Hunstanton through whom connection may be obtained with trunk service. The nearest ordinary telephone service is at Snettisham.

Water – Is at present obtained from a pump at a farm about a mile distant. This can only supply about 30 men, but there is a power pump and water tower about one mile distant which could possibly be arranged to supply the Aerodrome. The nearest watermains are, as far as I could ascertain, at Hunstanton (6 miles as the crow flies).

Light - At present all lighting is by oil. As far as I could ascertain the nearest power station is Hunstanton.

Road - There is a very poor road leading to the Aerodrome from the Sedgeford-Docking main road.

There are no houses or cottages for billets in the immediate vicinity. Sedgeford is ½ miles distant.

Malcolm Captain R.F.C., Commanding No. 9 Reserve Squadron R.F.C. Norwich

5th March 1916

45 Squadron

Following the changes to Britain's Home Defence system, R.N.A.S. stations such as those at Sedgeford and Narborough were transferred over to the R.F.C, with 45 Squadron being the first R.F.C. unit to be based at Sedgeford. The squadron was formed at Fort Grange, Gosport on 1st March, 1916, then moved up to Thetford on the 3rd May, before arriving at Sedgeford on the 21st May. The squadron was under the command of Captain C.E. Ryan and Major L.A. Strange. Major William Ronald Read M.C. was appointed on the 24th April 1916 to command the squadron, after having previously seen combat in France.

45 Squadron was part of network defence created to attack Zeppelins that had made it across the North Sea and into British airspace, the area around the Wash being a regular landfall for the German airships. The initial strategy for tackling any Zeppelin that crossed over to British soil relied heavily on the courage and bravery of British pilots. The advantage certainly lay with the Germans, with a Zeppelin having the advantage of height and speed and as many of these raids were at night, the airships proved extremely difficult to detect.

It was not only the fact that British pilots had difficulty in identifying a Zeppelin at night, the mere task to fly an aircraft at night was more than hazardous in itself. One problem that many night patrol pilots encountered during the initial stages of the Home Defence system was being able to read their own cockpit instruments; a fundamental requirement at any time. Problems such as these were among the many that were trying to be resolved with the evolving technology. The solutions were not always entirely satisfactory, as following instructions from the time in how to improve cockpit instrument visibility at night makes a suggestion.

'The machines will either be fitted with duplicate light sets for their instruments, or the pilot will take up an electric torch with him, if only one lighting set can be fitted'.

In the event that a pilot was lucky enough to locate a Zeppelin and get close enough to engage it, the pilot's problems were only just beginning. Aside from the fact that the Zeppelins themselves were heavily armed with a fearsome array of machine guns, the initial British tactic of attacking a Zeppelin involved firing a Hales grenade. The grenade itself launched from a standard service rifle and firing it involved fitting the grenade to the rifle, inserting the detonator, pulling back the safety pin collar, inserting a special blank round into the rifle, then firing. At the same time they had to try to keep the target in view and keep the aircraft flying!

At the start of the air defence campaign against the Zeppelin threat, R.F.C. pilots were further 'reassured' by receiving orders similar to the one that was issued to one squadron based on the outskirts of London:

> 'If the aeroplane fails to stop the airship by the time all ammunition is expended and the airship is still heading towards London, then the pilot must decide to sacrifice himself and his machine and ram the airship at the utmost speed'.

At Sedgeford, 45 Squadron always had an aircraft on standby in readiness to confront raiding Zeppelins. Additionally it also had a wireless unit on site that was engaged in listening for German airship communications.

Although its Home Defence responsibility was an important one, 45 Squadron's main role was to deliver advanced flying training for pilots in readiness for their transfer to France. Before arrival at Sedgeford, trainee pilots would have undertaken an induction course and then received their first taste of flying an aircraft with a reserve squadron. If the pilot was very fortunate, he may have spent ten hours in an aircraft learning how to fly it before he began his tactical training.

The training of British pilots, in advance of them being sent into combat at the Front, left much too be desired, particularly during the early years of the war. As a British pilot you were a third more likely to be killed during training, than during combat. Although detailed records remain imprecise, the number of pilots killed throughout the war years while engaged in training came to almost 8,000. This compares to just over 6,000 who were killed in combat.

During the spring of 1916, a new qualification was introduced aimed at improving the standard of pilot training. All pilots were to have flown solo for at least 15 hours, climbed to 6,000 feet and maintained that altitude for 15 minutes and flown an actual service plane (up until then trainee pilots often flew planes in training that they would not be using in combat). They had to make a cross-country flight of at least 60 minutes duration, which would also include two landings at R.F.C. airfields, along with making two night landings. In addition, pilots would be trained in landing, bombing, aerial fighting, night flying and formation flying.

Highlighting the hazardous and sometimes fatal risks of flight training, the pilots of 45 Squadron were involved in numerous accidents during their training at Sedgeford. Many of these accidents resulting in serious injuries to the pilots involved, including:

> 16th June, 1916 – 2nd Lt. James Ferme crashed his BE2c. Although he survived the crash he was unable to continue flying.
>
> 15th July, 1916 – 2nd Lt. R.H. Dawson was injured when the engine of his HF F20 stalled and he crashed into the ground.

20th July, 1916 – 2nd Lt. Gladstone crashed his BE2c. He too survived the crash but did not subsequently qualify as a pilot.

20th July, 1916 – 2nd Lt. G.L. Main was slightly injured after his BE2c crashed.

27th July, 1916 – F. Sgt. W.G. Webb was injured after the engine of his Martynside S1 seized and the aircraft crashed when he was forced to land.

23rd September, 1916 – 2nd Lt. E.E. Erlebach was injured when his Sopwith Strutter crash landed.

Two of the aircraft stationed at Sedgeford with 45 Squadron were fitted with radio transmitters which allowed trainee pilots to practice communicating with the radio receiver station on the ground. Pilots would also learn how to target artillery fire from the air using Morse code and, as the war developed, this was but one aspect of how the fledgling technology of aviation had been adapted to enhance the deadly effectiveness of the military machine. Training for targeting artillery involved a simulated target on the ground which would include a system of light bulbs, the pilots would then call in adjustments using a morse code telegraph key to adjust the accuracy of fire.

Another newfound role for pilots from the squadron when they reached the Front and commenced combat duties was photo reconnaissance. This was yet another function that had not existed at the outbreak of hostilities but had been developed and formulated as the war progressed. However, there appears to be no record of this being covered in detail during their training at Sedgeford.

45 Squadron was divided into three flights with a total of 18 aircraft; A Flight was commanded by Capt. G. Mountford, B Flight by Capt. E.F. P. Lubbock and C Flight by Capt. L. Porter. In addition, there were two Equipment Officers with responsibility for technical equipment, vehicles and radio, along with one Recording Officer.

Plate 5.3
An undated photograph of officers serving at Sedgeford aerodrome.

The following are some of 45 Squadron's pilots and crew:

Pilots	Observers
Lt. L.W. Arthur	Lt. F. Surgery
Lt. C.S.J. Griffin	2nd Lt. G.H. Bennett
Lt. L.A. Chamier	2nd Lt. W.J. Thuell
2nd Lt. A Chamier	2nd Lt. A.S. Carey
2nd Lt. H.G.P. Lowe	2nd Lt. N.G. Arnold
2nd Lt. E.G. Manuel	2nd Lt. C.S. Emery
2nd Lt. H.H. Griffith	2nd Lt. W. Jordan
2nd Lt. M.J. Fenwick	2nd Lt. F.H. Austin
2nd Lt. G.H. Cock	2nd Lt. G.B. Samuels
2nd Lt. V.B. Allen	2nd Lt. J.A. Vessey
2nd Lt. O.J. Wade	2nd Lt. F. Fullerton
2nd Lt. G.H. Rodwell	2nd Lt. D.E. Greenhow
2nd Lt. N.H. Read	Sgt. P.S. Taylor
2nd Lt. E.E. Glorney	**Ground Staff**
2nd Lt. L.F. Jones	Lt. R.C. Morgan (Rec. Officer)
F/Sgt. W.G. Webb	2nd Lt. L.R. Wright (W/T Officer)
Sgt. R.G. Malcolm	2nd Lt. T.H. Birdsall (AE Officer)
Sgt. P. Snowden	

Throughout the summer months of 1916, 45 Squadron's mobilisation preparations continued apace. Sopwith 1½ Strutters arrived, with pilots and crew honing their skills for their impending departure to France. On the 4th October a 49 vehicle convoy left Sedgeford, snaking its way along the country roads of Norfolk bound for St. Omer in France. The aircraft departed on the 12th October to join up with the rest of the British Expeditionary Force.

Plate 5.4
A Bristol Scout parked in front of flight sheds at Sedgeford.

64 Squadron

64 Squadron was formed at Sedgeford on the 1st August, 1916, its core coming from 45 Squadron, and was placed under the command of Major B.E. Smythies. The squadron initially undertook instructional flying using FE2b and Henri Farman aircraft. There was also a BE2c and two de Havillands of unknown type on site during this period. The squadron was re-designated for night flying training in June 1917 and with this change of role, received new aircraft in the shape of a flight of Henri Farmans, a flight of Sopwith Pups and in the following months, 18 DH5s.

Initially the squadron operated two flights; A Flight using Henri Farmans and the BE2c and B Flight using Henri Farmans and FE2b's. By September, A Flight was using 7 Henri Farmans and B Flight four FE2bs and a single DH. In November a third flight had been added, so the squadron's complement of aircraft consisted of A Flight – nine Henri Farmans, B Flight – five FE2bs, C Flight – one FE2b and two DHs.

It was during this period that the expansion of Sedgeford aerodrome really began. Personnel arriving to join 64 Squadron found accommodation at the airfield to be extremely limited, many officers being billeted at the nearby old Docking workhouse. Like many other training centres for other British forces, the pilots found the regime at Sedgeford a tough one, resulting in quite a high failure rate. A typical day's programme for 64 Squadron's officers would have resembled:

04.30 – Subject to orderly officer making decision as to weather allowing flying to take place, officers are called.
05.00 – Lorry leaves the workhouse billets.
05.15 – All personnel required to be at the aerodrome.
05.30 to 07.00 – Flying
07.00 to 07.30 – Breakfast. Officers returned to the workhouse for theirs. Ground crew to remain on site for theirs.
08.00 to 12.45 – All officers on aerodrome.
14.00 to dusk (flying days) – All officers at aerodrome
14.30 to 16.30 (non–flying days) – All officers at aerodrome.
19.30 – Dinner.

Plate 5.5
Officers from 64 Squadron. Photograph taken outside of their billet at the Burntstalks, Docking. The building was previously used as a workhouse.

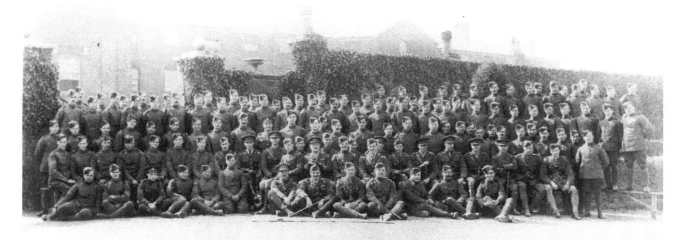

Throughout the war pilot training was an extremely dangerous and attritional undertaking. The technology being used was still relatively new and as such, very prone to mechanical and/or structural failure (this is not accounting for any human error in flying it). Attempting to learn to fly in a machine that stood a pretty good chance of failing on you was certainly not conducive to gaining confidence in the air. If this wasn't enough for a novice to deal with, trainee pilots also had to contend with another serious problem; their instructors. Many of these instructors had been sent back to Britain after seeing active service at the Front. In the majority of cases, the main reason for their return was that their nerves had been shredded during combat. Instead of being able to recuperate and recover from their ordeal, these young pilots were tasked with teaching others without having had any training themselves in the skill of teaching. For many of these novice instructors (some being as young as 18 years of age) the last thing that they wanted to do in any circumstance was to get back into an aircraft, let alone with a nervous student at the controls.

Plate 5.6
Service personnel based at Sedgeford posing for photograph outside one of the canvas tents used as temporary accommodation.

During this period pilot training could vary enormously, both in terms of flying time and the quality of instruction received. One such fledgling pilot to arrive at Sedgeford for training was Henry Samson Wolff (his middle name belying the fact that he was only five feet two inches tall!). Wolff had joined the Inns of Court Officers Training Corps in the Autumn of 1916, directly from school and shortly after he was commissioned into the Royal Flying Corps. After completing his induction training, he moved on to Reading to undergo theory of flight instruction. During April 1917 he was sent to Thetford for dual instruction, making his first solo flight after only four hours dual instruction. His posting to Sedgeford shortly followed, where after completing a variety of courses, he joined 64 Squadron. Appendix 1 is a copy of Wolff's flight log from his time at Sedgeford. His record shows the extent of his flying experience before receiving an overseas posting to Candas, France where he was subsequently posted to 40 Squadron.

Plate 5.7
An open day held at the aerodrome during the First World War.

Training at Sedgeford was both difficult and dangerous and not without incident. The following is a list of just some of the accidents that occurred during 64 Squadron's time there:

1st August, 1916 - Capt. E. Lubbock and 2nd Lt. A. Holden were both injured when the engine of their Henri Farman F20 (7437) failed at 50 feet and they crash landed.

17th August, 1916 - 2/AM D. Redford of A Flight had to force land his Henri Farman F20 into a nearby cornfield after engine failure. The aircraft finished up nose first into the ground. The pilot managed to escape unhurt but the aircraft suffered major damage and had to be written off.

18th August, 1916 - The following day, the same pilot stalled another Henri Farman F20 from a height of ten feet when coming into land. Again the pilot was unhurt but the aircraft suffered major damage to its undercarriage and wings.

18th August, 1916 - Also on the same day, Capt. E.F. P. Lubbock had taken up 2nd Lt. A. Holden in a Henri Farman F20. The aircraft had barely cleared the ground when a magneto lead came loose, causing the engine to stop. Taught never to turn during a stall, the aircraft continued straight on before crashing into a hedge at the perimeter of the airfield. Both pilots were thrown from the aircraft and were unharmed apart from Holden who sprained his wrist. The aircraft was a complete write off.

2nd September, 1916 - Lt. Purnell of the Royal Army Medical Corps was flying another Henri Farman F20 (7434). Turning at 200 feet, the aircraft stalled and went into a spinning nosedive. There appeared to be no fault in the machine or engine. The pilot had only had 40 minutes of solo flying experience. He survived the ensuing crash but fractured his left leg and injured his right ankle.

24th September, 1916 - 2nd Lt. W.S. Spence flying an FE2b (6957) was making a landing approach when he misjudged his altitude, inadvertently stopping his engine and performing a partial nosedive from twenty feet. He suffered facial injuries that required treatment at King's Lynn hospital. The aircraft was wrecked.

15th January, 1917 - 2nd Lt. J.W. van Alstyne flying a Henri Farman F20 (A1179) failed to flatten out upon landing and the nose of the aircraft struck the ground. The pilot was taken to King's Lynn hospital with leg injuries and the aircraft was written off.

7th February, 1917 - 2nd Lt. W. Dawson flying a Henri Farman F20 (7412) suffered engine trouble and was forced to land. As he landed, the pilot failed to flatten out and crashed. The aircraft was wrecked but the pilot managed to walk away from the crash but suffered shock.

8th February, 1917 - 2nd Lt. K.W. Brunsby stalled and crashed his Henri Farman F20 just after take off but escaped uninjured.

15th April, 1917 - 2nd Lt. E.F. Terry flying a Henri Farman F20 (A1189), crashed into a ploughed field close to the aerodrome after the engine blew an inlet valve, requiring him to make a forced landing in a cross wind. The pilot escaped badly shaken and bruised.

16th April, 1917 – 2nd Lt. L. Murray-Stewart was instructing 2nd Lt. H.S. Savage in a Henri Farman F20 (A1229), when Savage applied full rudder and full opposite bank, sending the aircraft into a spinning nose dive at 100 feet. Both instructor and pupil escaped from the crash badly shaken and with cuts and bruises. The pupil did not progress any further with his flying career after the crash.

6th May, 1917 – 2nd Lt. R.R. Harkus stalled his FE2b on taking off in a cross wind. The plane crashed into a nearby field and burst into flames. Fortunately the pilot was thrown clear and was taken to King's Lynn hospital suffering from concussion and shock.

Plates 5.8 and 5.9
The burnt out wreckage of an FE2b which stalled on take off and burst into flames upon impact on 6th May, 1917. The aircraft was piloted by 2nd Lt. R.R. Harkus of 64 Squadron, who miraculously escaped serious injury.

Towards the end of June the Squadron's role was to change, becoming a fighter squadron before leaving for France. The new focus was now on producing trained scout pilots. New aircraft were to be received, with a flight of Avro 504s, one flight of Sopwith Pups and eighteen DH5s arriving at Sedgeford. New personnel also arrived in the shape of three new flight commanders. A Canadian, Capt. E.R. Tempest who was in command of A Flight, Capt. R. St. Clair-McClintock commanded B Flight and Capt. James A. Slater commanded C Flight.

Trainee pilots commenced their training on the dual-control Avro 504, before moving on to the Sopwith Pup and finally advancing on to the DH5, where they were to hone their skills as scout pilots. In the main, their training consisted of air-to-ground gunnery, low-level flying and cross-country formation flying. Much of the gunnery practice took place at a range on the coastal marshes at nearby Thornham.

During this 'working up' period, training again was not without its accidents, some of which were to prove to be fatal:

8th August, 1917 - At 4.30pm, a Sopwith Pup (B1788) flown by a Canadian pilot 2nd Lt. A.L.R. Dean crashed into a field next to the Sedgeford-Docking road. The pilot had been practising spinning but appears to have lost control of his aircraft at a height of 500 feet, when it spiralled into the ground. Flight Sergeant A. Crowther happened to be cycling along the road close to where the aircraft crashed. He rushed to the scene and found Dean entangled in the wreckage of the aircraft. He was unable to extract the pilot and held him upright until assistance arrived. Dean was taken to King's Lynn hospital but died of his injuries the following day.

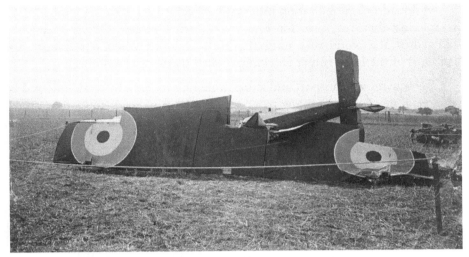

Plate 5.10
The wreckage of the Sopwith Pup (B1788) flown by Canadian pilot 2nd Lt. A.L.R. Dean of 64 Squadron, which crashed into a field next to the Sedgeford-Docking road on 8th August, 1917. The pilot died of his injuries in hospital the following day.

9th August, 1917 – Captain E.G. Hanlan, another Canadian pilot, had been performing aerial manoeuvres in a DH5 (A9393) for about an hour, when coming out of a loop the aircraft lost its upper starboard wing. The aircraft plummeted to the ground at Bircham Newton, instantly killing the pilot (however, an alternative record has the crash site being close to Docking Hall).

Capt. Hanlan was to receive full military honours at his funeral in Toronto, with thousands turning out to pay their respects. Major B.E. Smythies, Commander of 64 Squadron, wrote to Hanlan's sister:

> "While flying a fast De Havilland machine, practising aerial evolutions at a height of 7,000 feet, a portion of the wing broke and the machine became uncontrollable. The aviator made an attempt to regain control but this was not possible and the machine crashed to earth, and he was killed instantly. He had flown this same machine and looped with it two days before.
>
> He was a fine pilot and had the heart of a lion - he looped a Sopwith Scout on his first flight - he would have been going to France the next day. The Flying Corps lose a gallant officer and a really good scout pilot. He was killed instantaneously, the machine being in small fragments.
>
> In your sorrow you have my deep sympathy - he was killed while on duty under what is really active service conditions."

31st August, 1917 - 2nd Lt F.B.H. Anderson flying a Sopwith Pup (B1787), lost control of the aircraft at a height which did not enable him to recover. The aircraft descended in a spinning nosedive and crashed into the ground, with the pilot suffering multiple injuries. He was taken to King's Lynn hospital where he was to receive his wings shortly before dying on 3rd September.

Training continued apace at Sedgeford, as final preparations were made for the squadron's departure to France. Discipline appears to have been very stringent, with records showing that timekeeping in particular was strictly observed. The Squadron Office required a form to be completed showing details of each aircraft that took off – pilot name, aircraft type and serial number and take off time. All watches were synchronised daily with the clock outside the office.

64 Squadron's mobilisation orders were received on 30th September, 1917 instructing them to leave for France on 14th October. Officers remained billeted at the workhouse until the 10th October, when Mr Everitt, the landlord of the Hare Inn at Docking, cooked them a farewell meal.

The squadron's transport and stores were first to leave by road, followed by a party of mechanics traveling by rail. Finally on Sunday, 14th October, the 8 DH5s took off in their respective flights and after a refuelling stop at Lympne in Kent, crossed over the Channel to France.

53 Reserve Squadron

The 53 Reserve/Training Squadron was formed at Sedgeford on 1st February, 1917, with some of 64 Squadron having been re-designated into it. A range of aircraft were used, including: AMC DH6, Avro 504B, Avro 504 A/J, Be2c and RE8. The Squadron moved to Narborough on 14th February, 1917.

65 Reserve Squadron (later to become 65 Training Squadron)

65 Squadron was formed at Croydon on 1st May, 1917 and moved to Sedgeford, having been renamed the 65 Training Squadron, on the 10th May. Aircraft flown by the squadron included: Avro 504J, Armstrong Whitworth FK3, Armstrong Whitworth FK8, Bristol Scout D, Martynside G102, BE2e, RE8, Sopwith Pup and Sopwith Camel. Accidents which occurred during the squadron's time at Sedgeford included:

> 12th May, 1917 - Capt. E. G. Hanlan (who was killed later that year in a flying accident at Sedgeford) crashed after his Avro 504A got into too steep a climb and nosedived.
>
> 25th May, 1917 - 2nd Lt. H.G. Corby was injured when the engine failed on his Bristol Scout (A5209) and the aircraft crashed to the ground.
>
> 7th June, 1917 - 2nd Lt. R.J. Mark was injured after the engine of his DH5 (A9376) choked on take off and crashed.
>
> 25th July, 1917 - Lt. R Heath was injured after his Avro 504 A/J developed engine problems and crashed into trees.
>
> 8th August, 1917 - Capt. L. Whitehead was injured after his Sopwith Camel (B3849) crashed on take off.
>
> 16th September, 1917 - Lt. Parsons was injured flying an Avro 504A/J which went into a flat spin and nose dived from 60 feet.
>
> 3rd October, 1917 - 2nd Lt. A.B. Sneddon did not return from a training flight over the North Sea and was believed to have crashed and drowned.

The Squadron left for Dover on 25th November, 1917.

87 Squadron

Formed at Upavon on 1st September, 1917, the squadron moved to Sedgeford on 15th September, operating under the command of Capt. C.J.W. Darwin. Training as a fighter unit while at Sedgeford, the squadron moved to Hounslow on 19th December, 1917, before joining the British Expeditionary Force at St. Omer in April the following year. Aircraft used by the squadron included: Avro 504J, SE5a, Sopwith Pup, Sopwith Camel and Sopwith Dolphin. During the squadron's period at Sedgeford, the only accident recorded being:

> 15th November, 1917 - Lt. J.S. Walser was injured when the Avro 504J (B4252) he was flying while training, spun into the ground, writing off the aircraft.

72 Squadron

Formed at Upavon on 28th June, 1917. After moving to Netheravon on 8th July, the squadron arrived at Sedgeford on 1st November, 1917 to train as a fighter squadron. Commanded by Major H.W. von Poellintz, the squadron's other officers had been posted to France, so replacements were sent for to start mobilisation for the campaign in the Middle East. The 72 Squadron departed Sedgeford for Mesopotamia on 25th December, 1917. Aircraft used by the squadron included: Avro 504A, Sopwith Pup and a SPAD S. VII. The only recorded accident during the squadron's stay at Sedgeford being:

> 3rd December, 1917 - Lt J. Lawson was injured when his Avro 504J (B3123) crashed on take off. 2nd Lt. R.W. Stower, who was also in the aircraft, escaped injury.

110 Squadron

110 Squadron was formed at Rendcomb on 1st November, 1917, moving to Sedgeford on the 26th of that month from Swingate Down, Dover. Under the command of Major H.R. Nicholl, pilots undertook training as a light bomber squadron.

Plate 5.11
The mangled wreckage of 2nd Lt. J.A. Pearson's Martinsyde G100 (B866) which crashed, killing the pilot, on 9th December, 1917

While at Sedgeford, the squadron was to suffer two fatalities during training:

> 9th December, 1917 - 2nd Lt. J.A. Pearson was too late out of a dive and the tail of the Martinsyde G100 (B866) he had been flying collapsed at 1500 feet. Pearson fell out of the cockpit, falling to his death.

17th February, 1918 - 2nd Lt. F.B. Evans was killed when the DH4 (B9994) he was flying on a training flight caught fire. It was not possible to identify the cause of the fire which caused his death. The *Norfolk Chronicle*, dated 22nd February, 1918, includes the following account of the inquest into the accident:

'2nd Lt. Francis Bernard Evans was 22 years old at the time of his death. One officer said that he had been instructing him and after landing had sent Evans up alone in another type of machine. He described him as "quite a good pilot and had done over sixty hours flying alone in other types of machine". Another officer said that he saw the machine landing and that it was on fire, apparently from under the engine. Evans glided the machine down and when about 20 feet from the ground the machine nose dived and burst into flames. The report speculates that Evans was unaware that the machine was on fire until he had nearly reached the ground. A verdict of accidental death was recorded.'

Other accidents to occur during the squadron's time at Sedgeford included:

20th April, 1918 - A DH9 flown by 2nd Lt. R.G. Young and 2nd Lt. A.F. Tong, stalled during a turn and nosed dived to the ground. The crash severely injured Young, with Tong sustaining minor injuries.

23rd April, 1918 - Another DH9 (C6071) flown by Lt. H.V. Brisbin and Lt. Phillips, stalled and fell into a spinning nose dive. The crash severely injured Brisbin, with Phillips picking up minor injuries.

15th May, 1918 - 2nd Lt. R.T. Finks side slipped his Armstrong Whitworth FK3 (B9643) and in the subsequent crash he sustained severe injuries.

21st May, 1918 - Capt. G.J. MacLean and 1st Airman E.A.E. Hart were both injured when the tail folded on their DH9 (C6089), causing the aircraft to crash.

During their training at Sedgeford, 110 Squadron's pilots undertook a series of lectures which covered a wide range of technical and theoretical skills:

Weekly Programme of Lectures for w/e 9-2-18
No 110 Squadron Royal Flying Corps

Date	Subject	Lecturer	Place	Time
Sunday				
Monday	Photography	Maj. R.R. Nicholl	Ante-room	5.30 - 6.30pm
Tuesday	Cross country	Capt. Vincent	Ante-room	-do-
Wednesday	Bombs	Bombing Officer	Buzzing Room	12. - 12.30pm
Thursday	Bomb raids/ Escort	Capt.N.N. Pearson	Ante-room	5.30 - 6.00pm
Friday	Aerobatics	Capt. S.F. Vincent	-do-	-do-
Saturday	Compasses	2nd Lt. Vane-Hunt	-do-	-do-

Weekly Programme of Lectures for w/e 2-3-18
No 110 Squadron Royal Flying Corps

Date	Subject	Lecturer	Place	Time
Sunday				
Monday	Photography	2nd. Lt. Kurn	Ante-room	5.00 - 5.30pm
Tuesday	Cross country	Lt. Brisbin	-do-	-do-
Wednesday	Bombs	Bombing Officer	Buzzing Room	12 - 12.30pm
Thursday	Formation Flying	Capt. K.S.P. Carson	Ante-room	5.00 - 5.30pm
Friday	General	Maj. R.R. Nicholl	-do-	-do-
Saturday	Compasses	2nd Lt. Vane-Hunt	-do-	-do-

On the 15th June, 1918 the Squadron moved to Kenley.

Plate 5.12
2nd Lt. Charles Eaton of 9th Training School in his FE2b in front of G.S. Shed 1 at Sedgeford.

Plates 5.13, 5.14 and 5.15
Unidentified aircraft crashes at Sedgeford.

122 Squadron

122 Squadron was formed at Sedgeford on the 1st January, 1918 as a day bomber unit. The squadron came under the command of Major A.S.C. MacLaren but did not become operational and was subsequently disbanded at Sedgeford on 17th August, 1918. Aircraft used by the Squadron included - AMC DH6, AMC DH9, Armstrong Whitworth FK3, Martinsyde G.102, RE8.

9 Training Squadron

Formed at Mousehold Heath, Norwich on 27th July, 1915, the squadron made the short journey across Norfolk, arriving at Sedgeford on 10th January, 1918. The squadron operated as the 7th Wing of No. 3 Training Group. Aircraft used by the squadron included: AMC DH1A, AMC DH4, Avro 504D, Armstrong Whitworth FK3, Caudron G.III, Henri Farman F.20, Martinsyde S.1, MF Se.7, MF Se11, BE2c, BE2d, BE2e, FE2b, RE8, Vickers FB5.

A communique summarising the work carried out by No. 3 Training Group, sheds some light on the operational performance of the 7th Wing during the summer of 1918. It appears that the weather was exceptionally kind throughout the summer months, with all stations taking advantage of the fine weather and a total of 92,952 hours were flown at the Group's ten stations. At Sedgeford, pilots flew 4,690 hours during May, 3,191 hours in June, 3,454 hours in July and 902 hours in August (the 7th Wing was disbanded during this month).

During May and early June, much of a trainee pilot's flight instruction was undertaken using DH6 or RE8 aircraft, with pupils only getting a short time on a service type of machine due to shortages. By the end of June the shortage appears to have been rectified and July saw all pupils putting in at least twelve hours on service aircraft.

In the period of the establishment of the 3rd Training Group, there had been a significant shortage of instructors and this situation appears not to have been resolved until August, 1918. Training squadrons, such as those at Sedgeford, sorely lacked Flight Commanders and Instructors who had gained the valuable combat experience which could be passed on to pupils. A programme of producing assistant instructors was started at Sedgeford and during the summer, the 7th Wing turned out 26 Assistant Instructors. A further four Instructors were sent on courses at the School of Special Flying.

Throughout the summer, the 9th Training Squadron at Sedgeford turned out the following numbers of qualified pilots: May - 23, June – 15, July – 25, August - 19. Again, the training programme was not without incidents and the following accidents occurred at Sedgeford during this period:

> 27th July, 1918 - 2nd Lt. John Todd, a pilot under instruction, was killed at 3.10 pm when he turned his RE8 without sufficient speed, resulting in a nosedive from which he did not have sufficient height to recover.
>
> 8th September, 1918 - A DH4 (A7793) piloted by Lieutenant H.H. Cotton stalled in a turn and nose-dived into the ground from 100ft

in failing light. The falling aircraft landed on Capt. Selbil Macneill Campbell, killing him instantly.

The communique further highlights a problem shared by many aerodromes at the time, in that they suffered from not being able to obtain enough suitable sites which could be used for aerial firing practice. Because of land being required for agricultural use, much of the practice took place on the aerodrome site itself which gave less than satisfactory results. From May to August, the 7th Wing fired 200,652 rounds as part of their aerial firing training.

In addition to aerial firing, pilots also learned how to operate the camera gun which was used for photo reconnaissance. It was here that the lack of instructors with combat experience was felt the most, with many pupils struggling to obtain the correct levels of exposure until suitable instructors were brought in. Photo reconnaissance had evolved into an enormously powerful strategic tool and by the final year of the war both sides were photographing the entire front twice a day.

The 3rd Training Group managed to establish a site for live bombing practice at Lakenheath, which in addition to having a dozen targets marked out in chalk on the ground, also had a landing ground nearby so that pilots could reload. Throughout the summer the Group dropped over 45 tons of bombs during their training, with pilots from Sedgeford dropping a total of 1,110 bombs. Navigation was another area that initially encountered problems through lack of instructors, there only being three in the entire Group when it was formed, and also through a lack of equipment. The report mentions that the photographic training encountered problems with mist but this did not stop pilots at Sedgeford taking 6,459 printable negatives between May and August.

The Squadron left Sedgeford in August, 1918 for Tallaght, Ireland.

24 Aero Squadron

The 24 Aero Squadron left the United States aboard the Cunard Liner RMS *Carmania*, arriving in Liverpool on 24th January, 1918. It then travelled by train to Romney Rest Camp at Winchester where it was assigned to the Royal Flying Corps for advanced training. The squadron was divided into four flights, C Flight being sent to Sedgeford on 31st January, 1918. C Flight was attached to 9 Training Squadron, where American personnel worked with the British in maintaining aircraft and learning the means and methods of an operational squadron. On 1st May, 1918 all flights were reassembled as a complete squadron at Narborough for final training.

3 Fighting School

Fighting Schools were established with the objective of providing pilots with combat techniques training in advance of them being sent into operational service. Originally formed as 3 School of Aerial Fighting & Gunnery at Driffield in May 1918, the school had moved to Bircham Newton on 29th May. It then moved to Sedgeford as 3 Fighting School during November 1918.

3 Fighting School's Commanding Officer was Major Harold Harrington Balfour. When not overseeing operations at Bircham Newton and Sedgeford, he would spend much of his spare time fly fishing at Hillington Hall, near Bircham, which had been opened to R.F.C. and R.A.F. officers. Balfour also maintained that he undertook the first naked flight over Hunstanton, after having gained the inspiration for it after going nude bathing at a beach near Brancaster.

At this particular point in time there must have been something in the water at Sedgeford that brought out the extrovert in pilots. Another famous instance of a pilot performing extraordinary feats was that of Capt. Jimmy Slater. Slater had been posted to Sedgeford with 64 Squadron in 1917, where he commanded C Flight. He returned from France in July, 1918, having become a fighter ace with 22 victories in total, to be assigned as an Instructor at Sedgeford. Accounts suggest that one of his speciality pieces was to fly his aircraft through the open doors of a hangar and out the other side. During the summer of that year, Queen Alexandra visited the aerodrome from nearby Sandringham and Slater was asked to put on a display for the royal guest. Slater had been only airborne a few minutes before the Queen instructed the Commanding Officer to 'Order that young man down before he kills himself'. It also appears that Slater took great delight in flying over Hunstanton at chimney pot height at 8 o'clock on Saturday mornings, visiting each of his girlfriends' houses!

It was during the unit's period of operation at Sedgeford that the Royal Air Force was formed on the 1st April, 1918. At Sedgeford pupils (pilots who had graduated at level B from their respective training stations) would be taught a finishing course that would allow them to pass out as a service pilot. The course itself was a combination of aerial gunnery and aerial fighting modules, which included:

'The advanced use of sights, guns and gears, both on the ground and in the air.

Advanced formation flying at service heights, and low formation flying in the case of Scout pilots.

Fighting in the air, at first dual control with an instructor, then one pupil against another and finally pupil against instructor and Scouts against two-seaters.'

The school at Sedgeford had a capacity for 160 pupils, with each course lasting three weeks, although during October, 1918 the school appears to be operating at only half-strength.

A summary report on the School produced during that month, puts the number of personnel at the aerodrome as follows:

Officers	61
Officers under instruction	204
W.O's and N.C.O's above the rank of Corporal	72
Corporals	68
Rank and File	597
Boys	8
Women	145

Women (Household)   60
TOTAL   1,215

The same report also includes a meteorological report for the months October, 1917 to March, 1918, listing 1,926 daylight hours being observed.

Low Cloud Hours	Rainfall Hours	Wind Hours	Mist Hours	Fog Hours	Poss. Flying Hours	Total Daylight Hours Observed	Ratio of Poss. Flying to Daylight Hours	Category
193.5	344.5	394.5	128.5	68	1,058	1,926	54.93	2

It was during 3 Fighting School's residency at Sedgeford that the aerodrome was to undergo substantial development. The aerodrome's buildings and infrastructure was already that of a substantial two squadron station and during the summer the aerodrome underwent significant expansion to bring it up to a three squadron station. The story of this development is covered in a later chapter on the archaeology of the site but by October 1918 work on the expansion scheme was well underway. A new railway spur had been added to the Heacham to Wells line during the months of July through to September. The rail link would allow supplies (including the building materials for the new development) to be received on site far quicker. The survey carried out in October highlighted that the status of constructing new aircraft sheds as being only 20% complete, regimental buildings 7.5% complete and road construction had barely started. However, all scheduled work was due to be completed by 1st January, 1919. During the summer months, the influx of additional personnel at Sedgeford applied significant pressure on the site's infrastructure, with living quarters in particular being in very short supply. Two of the Motor Transport (M.T.) sheds and the old naval hangar were converted into sleeping quarters. Even during the preceding months, accommodation at Sedgeford had been at a premium, with many of the personnel living in tents sited around the aerodrome.

The aircraft used by 3 Fighting School included: DH1A, DH4, Avro 504D, Armstrong Whitworth FK3, Caudron G.III, Henri Farman F.20, Martinsyde S.1, MF Se.7, MF Se.11, BE2c, BE2d, BE2e, FE2b, RE8 and the Vickers FB5.

After the signing of the Armistice on the 11th November, 1918, everyday life still carried on at Sedgeford, with pilots continuing their training. Unfortunately, much as they had done during previous years, accidents were still to occur on a regular basis:

> 24th October, 1918 - 2nd Lt. Henry Birkett was flying as a passenger with his instructor Lt. Marks in an Avro 504K. The weather had not been good enough for pupils to go out but good enough for instructors. The aircraft had been in the air for about five or ten minutes, with witnesses seeing the machine flying at about 100 feet. The pilot then shut off his engine and started a sharp left turn. In doing the turn, the pilot put on too much left rudder; the machine stalled and turned over on to its back. There was insufficient time to bring the aircraft out of the resulting nosedive and it crashed vertically into the ground. Witnesses arriving at the scene of the crash found Birkett in the front seat and Marks in the rear. Marks

escaped uninjured but Birkett was killed instantly, suffering serious chest injuries. Examination of the controls found them all to be in working order.

18th November, 1918 - 2nd Lt. Jack Garside was killed when his Sopwith Camel crashed.

24th January, 1919 - Captain C.F. King M.C., D.F.C. and Croix de Guerre, was flying a Sopwith Camel which collided with another Sopwith Camel flown by 2nd Lt. H.C. Daniel M.C., there having been several machines in the air at the time of the collision. Witnesses saw each plane collide into each other, with both appearing to be in each other's blind spot. King's aircraft was the more seriously damaged and it plunged to the ground with him being unable to regain control. Daniel managed to land his aircraft safely back at the aerodrome.

At the inquest into King's death, Lt. H.C. Daniels said that he had been flying in formation, with Capt. King on the inside right. King had dived and then zoomed, which was the pre-arranged wash-out signal. When King dived again, Daniels followed him for about 100 feet, then flattened out and flew straight. Two seconds after that he felt something hit his machine on the front, which put Daniels' machine out of control. He managed to stay in the aircraft and regain control and land on the aerodrome.

Capt. F.H. Wallace, the aerodrome's medical officer also gave evidence at the inquest. He described how he had been called to examine King's body and found that he had suffered a fractured skull, a broken jaw and broken left arm and left leg. His death had been instantaneous.

Aged only19 years and 11 months, King had achieved a very distinguished military career by the time of his death. After leaving Charterhouse school early in 1917 to join the Royal Flying Corps, he was sent to France in September of the same year. He achieved 22 victories, of which 19 were confirmed. He had only recently been transferred to Sedgeford as a fighting instructor at the time of his death.

2nd February, 1919 - 2nd Lt. Percy Heathers, a Canadian serving with the R.A.F. died when he crashed his Sopwith Camel at Sedgeford. At the inquest, Capt. J.L. White described how he had been flying in formation with Heathers at 5,000 feet. Suddenly Heathers aircraft dropped to 500 feet and then stalled and went into a spin before crashing into the ground. White stated that Heathers had not previously done any high flying and he thought that the numbing effect of cold air at 5,000 feet may have had an effect on him, with the sudden drop causing him to faint. An inspection of the aircraft found it to be in good working order. Heather suffered multiple injuries, including multiple broken bones, and was admitted to King's Lynn hospital where he later died of shock caused by his injuries.

On the 14th March, 1919, the unit was re-designated 7 Training Squadron.

13 Squadron Cadre

Formed at Gosport on the 10th January, 1915, the squadron left for France in October of the same year. After the cessation of hostilities, 13 Squadron arrived, without their aircraft, at Sedgeford from St. Omer on 27th March, 1919. The squadron was disbanded on 31st December, 1919.

60 Squadron

Formed at Gosport on 30 April, 1916, the squadron was almost immediately sent to France. After the Armistice the squadron began to demobilise while still in France, with most of the officers and men who remained being sent by train as reinforcements for the R.A.F. with the Army of the Rhine. It was left for the remaining two officers and ten men of the cadre to return by trucks through the snow to Sedgeford on 28th February, 1919. The unit was disbanded on 22nd January, 1920.

7 Training School

The unit was re-designated from 3 Fighting School at Sedgeford on 14th March, 1919. It was disbanded in October of the same year.

Grave of 2nd Lt. A.L.R. Dean   Capt. E. G. Hanlan   Grave of Capt. E. G. Hanlan

Capt. C. King   Grave of Capt. C. King   Grave of 2nd Lt. J.A. Pearson

Plate 5.16
Service personnel killed at Sedgeford

With

Best Wishes

for Xmas and the New Year

From

Royal Flying Corps.
Sedgeford.
Kings Lynn.
Norfolk.

Plate 5.17
Undated Christmas card sent from Sedgeford aerodrome.

Chapter 6

The Archaeology of the Aerodrome

The Sedgeford Historical and Archaeological Research Project (SHARP) was established in 1996 as a long-term, multi-period research project. Its primary objective being to investigate the entire range of human settlement and land use in Sedgeford, a typical Norfolk parish. Since then, SHARP has developed into one of the largest and longest running independent archaeological research projects in the UK. From its genesis, the project's research has been focussed on the earlier periods of Sedgeford's intriguing history but in 2009 SHARP began to undertake field-based and desktop research of Sedgeford aerodrome.

Since then, a small, enthusiastic team of volunteers have been working at the site, recording some of the remaining standing buildings and features and also trying to compile details of some of the personnel who served there. The following chapter is a description of the research that SHARP has undertaken thus far. Work which would not have been possible without the kind support of the landowner; research that is still ongoing and revealing new understanding of the site each year.

SHARP's research has been informed from a broad range of sources; the use of original aerial photographs and maps, personal records, anecdotal evidence from members of the local community and through field survey of the landscape; particularly after the undergrowth has died back and the remains of building structures and features are exposed.

Archaeological research is a continual process that requires ongoing evaluation and our work at Sedgeford aerodrome has been no different. Several features and their dating have been reappraised since their original recording and it is entirely likely that others mentioned in this chapter will also undergo re-evaluation in the future when assessed against new sources of evidence.

Today the aerodrome site is like many other past military aviation sites; either in part of totally turned over to agricultural or light industrial use. Several of the original standing buildings at Sedgeford still survive today, as do many of the foundation features of others. However, the footprints of many of the timber-framed buildings and features that once formed a large part of the site have been lost forever. Intensive ploughing of adjacent fields over many years has removed any trace of these buildings, that at best where ephemeral due to their temporary nature.

The site layout of the WWI aerodrome at Sedgeford does not directly fit that of other Training Depot Stations. From its initial role as a R.N.A.S. landing ground, the site grew organically and unlike other 'new build' stations which were constructed in a complete phase. Another factor disrupting its layout has been the Whin Close woodland, which rather than be cleared was built around. The topography of the land, as it falls away into the Heacham River valley, also placed restraints on the site layout.

The following is an attempt to put the development of the site phase during WWI into archaeological phases; from its origins in August,1915 as an R.N.A.S. landing ground, through to its significant expansion as a three squadron airfield at the time of the Armistice. The details of the buildings and features have been complied from excavation and on site survey and recording, along with recourse to documentary archives such as aerial photographs, squadron records and post-war auction lists. The documentary archive for the site is modest compared to others of the period and research continues which will refine our picture of how the aerodrome would have looked and operated during this period.

Phases have been applied where firm documentary evidence has been available to support the archaeological record. Usually, archaeological phasing reports on such buildings and features would combine specific information on finds recovered during the excavation and recording process. In this instance the phasing covers a period of just over four years, making the application of exact dating to within individual years for many of the finds discovered extremely difficult. As such, the finds are covered separately from the buildings and features listed, unless specific dating was obtained.

Three phasing periods have been used for the aerodrome during WWI; 1915 to 1916, 1917 and 1918. These periods cover the buildings and features which have been recorded to each phase. Some of the features are present across all phases, their presence is noted in later phases and the original description referred to unless having undergone significant change.

Phase 1 (1915 to 1916)

The aerodrome originally started life during August 1915 as an R.N.A.S. landing ground. No documentary or photographic evidence is available for the site during initial period. The earliest record of the site's buildings and features comes in an R.F.C. evaluation report, dated 5th March, 1916, produced prior to the arrival of 45 Squadron. A map of the site, dated 1916, is thought to have been produced shortly after the arrival of the R.F.C. The following buildings and features were known to have been in use on the site during this phase:

R.N.A.S. Flight Shed

A timber flight shed (measuring 66 feet x 52 feet) without a floor, was situated on the southern perimeter of the Whin Close woodland. As with

Fig. 6.1
Site plan of Sedgeford
aerodrome during 1916

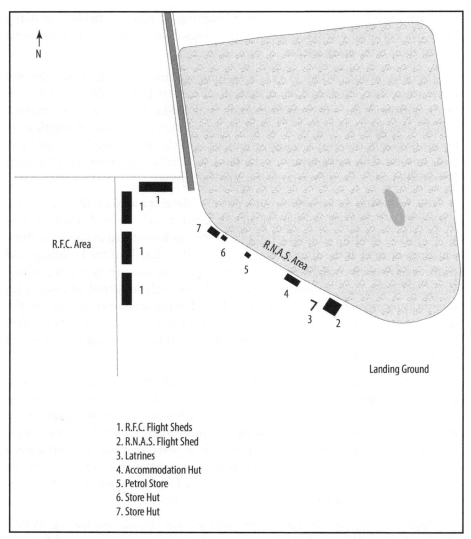

Fig. 6.1
Site plan of Sedgeford
aerodrome during 1916

many features from this period that were located in this area, reutilisation of the area for later buildings and the subsequent encroachment of the woodland has meant that is has not been possible to locate any evidence for this building, although an aerial photo from September, 1917 does show a vacant area that approximates to the flight shed's dimensions.

Latrines

Located along the southern perimeter of Whin Close, an area now covered under dense woodland. No details are available from the documentary record and no archaeological evidence has been recorded of this feature.

Accommodation Hut

A timber framed hut accommodated 17 airmen and three officers. Exact details of its dimensions are not available but a building resembling the accommodation hut appears on a September, 1917 aerial photograph with approximate dimensions of 60 feet x 15 feet. A building resembling the accommodation hut and in the same location appears on aerial photographs throughout the aerodrome's active life but no archaeological evidence has been recorded and it has not been possible to determine the building's purpose in its reused form in later phases.

Petrol Store

A petrol store is mentioned in the 5th March, 1916 evaluation report. No description or dimensions are given. It is thought that a larger fuel store, located close to the south west boundary of the site replaced this feature when the aerodrome expanded in late 1916/early 1917.

Storage Huts

Five timber framed storage huts are listed as being on the original R.N.A.S. site, with dimensions of 6 feet x 5 feet. Evidence for these features has not been located.

Bessonneau Hangar

A single Bessonneau hangar was recorded as being on the site. In March 1916, it was mentioned as being without a cover and under repair. This type of hangar was originally designed in France in 1908 but variants were adopted by the British forces throughout the war. It was largely made using a timber framework with a canvas cover and opening at one end. Two main types were in use at British aerodromes, both having a width of 64 feet, with a 6 bay version measuring 80 feet in length and a 9 bay version measuring 118 feet. The hangars could be quickly taken down and reassembled by a team of 20 skilled men at a new location within 48 hours. Due to their design, the structures left a very ephemeral archaeological footprint. However, copper alloy eyelets of varying sizes have been recovered within the area to the south of the Whin Close woodland, close to where this and subsequent Bessonneau hangars were located.

R.F.C. Twin Flight Sheds

The map produced in 1916 shows four twin flight sheds (also known as a Type B hangar) located to the west of the R.N.A.S. area. We do not have an exact date for their arrival but these are believed to be the first dedicated R.F.C. buildings to have arrived on the site and would have likely coincided with the arrival of 45 Squadron on 21st May 1916. The map shows the four sheds in the exact location as they appear in later aerial photos and it is believed that the sheds remained on site until at least 1919.

The 1916 map shows three of the buildings aligned north-south and a further one east-west, bordering the boundary of the north-west corner of the site. A single shed was 60 feet wide and 40 feet in length, with a clear opening height of 15 feet. The coupled buildings were constructed entirely from timber, having an earth floor, with timber posts spaced at 11 feet 3 inch intervals, each post supporting wooden trusses. Both walls and roof were clad with timber boarding. From the close positioning of the twin sheds at Sedgeford, it would appear that it would not be possible to operate sliding doors at the front of building, due to overlapping against the adjacent shed. It was likely that canvas doors were used instead. Aerial photos also show external timber braces along each side elevation to support the walls and roof trusses. The rear elevation of the sheds usually incorporated large louvred air vents under the gable end, although these are not directly identifiable on the Sedgeford buildings. In addition, twin doors are located in the rear elevation of each shed.

As discussed later in this chapter, an original flight shed still survives today in the nearby village of Heacham. Survey of the shed shows much of the original elevations to still be in place, although it has not been possible to inspect the rear of the building. The original roof has been replaced and a new frontage incorporated. The surviving shed has a series of metal framed windows aligned along each exterior side elevation, although interestingly these do no not appear on aerial photos of the buildings on site. Dating of the window frames has not been possible at the time of writing, although they appear to be of early 20th century design. The interior of the building has the original half-height interior wall, partioning the length of the shed to create a series of smaller work areas.

Phase 2 (1917)

By 1917 the aerodrome had undergone substantial development. During the autumn of 1916, the aerodrome became host to two R.F.C squadrons and saw significant growth in terms of both numbers and types of buildings on site. Like many other WWI aerodromes, the site was divided into two main areas; the Technical and Regimental. These two areas within a typical aerodrome of the period were generally separated. These building types also tended to differ in their construction design and materials; the Technical buildings typically were built on concrete foundations, with brick walls and tiled roofing, whereas Regimental buildings were usually timber framed and built on brick plinths.

The Technical Buildings

Dope Shop

In 2011, surveying began on some of the buildings originally sited in the western technical area along the south western boundary of the site. It is believed that all buildings within the western technical area of the site were cleared during 1919. The clearance of these buildings following auction was a fastidious one, with all material removed apart from their concrete foundations. The roadway that originally accessed this row of buildings is now just a narrow, overgrown grass track, with mature trees and dense undergrowth obscuring the foundations of the buildings that once stood here. One of these buildings was the dope shop, a building dedicated to the repair of aircraft wings and body. The standard dimensions for this type of building was 40 feet x 28 feet.

Fig. 6.3
Plan of dope shop recorded in western technical area of the site.

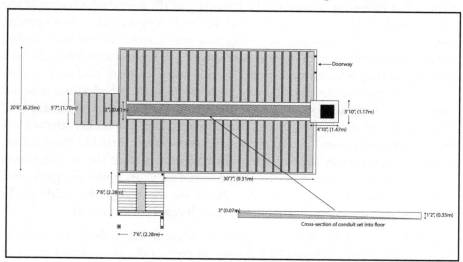

The dope shop building's purpose was to repair and reproof canvas-covered aircraft sections. The fabric covering the aircraft required protection from damp and a cellulose acetate dope called Emaillite was generally used for this purpose. Oil sprayed from the engine when in flight would have quickly deteriorated the fabric. An aircraft in general use would have required redoping every six months. Holes to the fabric would require immediate attention, with strips of fabric doped over small holes while larger holes would need a patch to be sewn in. In the event of accident, new wings or airframes would require treatment.

Plate 6.1
Interior floor of dope shop building in western technical area of the Sedgeford site. The conduit let into the floor to help express noxious fumes can be seen in the centre of the photograph.

Working in the dope shop would not be the most sought after job at the aerodrome. At the outset of the war, a substance called tetrachlorethane was used in the dope as part of the aircraft manufacturing process. It was soon to be found to be causing severe cases of toxic jaundice, often leading to fatalities. The substance was not banned until September 1916 but the job of doping aircraft still remained a hazardous one. Working instructions stated that fabric workers should always work in pairs and for only limited time periods.

One particular feature of this building drew immediate attention; an unusual H-shaped concrete pedestal, featuring curved surfaces when seen in section. The pedestal would have been contained within an annexe to the main dope shop building. The annexe measured 6 feet 8 inches x 10 feet 6 inches, and was attached to the north west corner of the dope shop. The annexe originally contained a large centrifugal, electric fan which was used to help ventilate the dope shop and help lessen the effect of inhaling dangerous chemicals. In vapour form, cellulose acetate was heavier than air, so a ventilation system was incorporated into the dope shop's construction which allowed these low-lying fumes to be expressed.

Plate 6.2
Annexe adjoining the dope shop building. The concrete pedestal was used as a mount for the electric centrifugal fan which helped to ventilate the building. The floor of the passageway which would have connected the dope shop to the adjacent workshop can be seen in the upper left of the photograph.

The large fan would have inserted fresh air into the building and pushed the noxious fumes through a concrete lined duct under the floor and up and out through a chimney flue at the southern end of the building. During the recording of the building, a small metal plate was found which bore the name Blackman Motor No. 52033. Further research revealed that the firm of James Keith Blackman Ltd, a company registered in Manchester and formed in 1900 by a merger of James Keith Ltd of Arbroath, Scotland with Blackman Ventilation Co. of Illinois, USA, made extractor fans for power stations before WWI. The Blackman branch of the company manufactured electric centrifugal fans. This probably explains the 220V rating on the identity plate as

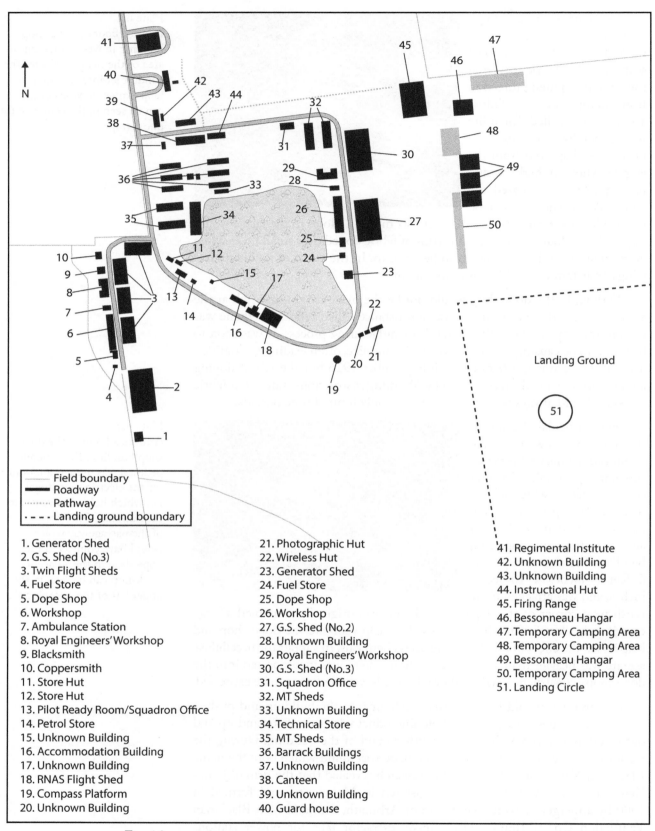

N

Legend:
—— Field boundary
▬ Roadway
········ Pathway
- - - Landing ground boundary

Landing Ground

1. Generator Shed
2. G.S. Shed (No.3)
3. Twin Flight Sheds
4. Fuel Store
5. Dope Shop
6. Workshop
7. Ambulance Station
8. Royal Engineers' Workshop
9. Blacksmith
10. Coppersmith
11. Store Hut
12. Store Hut
13. Pilot Ready Room/Squadron Office
14. Petrol Store
15. Unknown Building
16. Accommodation Building
17. Unknown Building
18. RNAS Flight Shed
19. Compass Platform
20. Unknown Building

21. Photographic Hut
22. Wireless Hut
23. Generator Shed
24. Fuel Store
25. Dope Shop
26. Workshop
27. G.S. Shed (No.2)
28. Unknown Building
29. Royal Engineers' Workshop
30. G.S. Shed (No.3)
31. Squadron Office
32. MT Sheds
33. Unknown Building
34. Technical Store
35. MT Sheds
36. Barrack Buildings
37. Unknown Building
38. Canteen
39. Unknown Building
40. Guard house

41. Regimental Institute
42. Unknown Building
43. Unknown Building
44. Instructional Hut
45. Firing Range
46. Bessonneau Hangar
47. Temporary Camping Area
48. Temporary Camping Area
49. Bessonneau Hangar
50. Temporary Camping Area
51. Landing Circle

Fig. 6.2
Site plan of Sedgeford
aerodrome 1917

Plate 6.3
Vertical aerial photograph
of Sedgeford aerodrome
(4th September, 1917). Two
squadrons were operating
from the site at this date.
Annotations show buildings
for 64 and 65 Squadrons.
The respective technical area
buildings can be seen to the
left of the photograph and
along the right of the Whin
Close woodland.

Plate 6.4
Vertical aerial photograph
taken by 64 Squadron during
1917. The twin flight sheds
and G.S. Shed No. 3 can be
seen adjacent to the western
technical area buildings
(from left to right - dope
shop, workshop, ambulance
station, R.E. workshop and
blacksmith).

Plate 6.5
Manufacturer's engine
plate for dope shop electric
centrifugal fan.

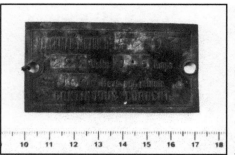

Plate 6.5
Manufacturer's engine
plate for dope shop electric
centrifugal fan.

that being the standard mains voltage in the USA.

The exhaust conduit within the dope shed building was inclined at a north to south angle and would have originally been covered by a timber cover. The floor of the dope shop was made from narrow concrete beams which were laid horizontally with a small aperture left between each one. The floor had then been coated with bitumen, forming narrow ducts between the blocks. The ducts lead into the central conduit, which measured 2 feet in width. Official plans for dope shop buildings which were constructed after the buildings at Sedgeford, show that twin exhaust conduits were laid into the flooring which conjoin when reaching the chimney block. Postholes for a double-width door were located in the south-east corner of the building.

The dope shop was linked to the workshop building to its north by a pathway, measuring 6 feet 6 inches in length and 5 feet 10 inches wide. The pathway was constructed using a series of concrete beams which had been coated in bitumen, similar to that of the main dope shop floor. A similar building has been found at Stow Maries, Essex and been completely renovated; here the buildings are linked by an enclosed passageway, with double-width doors opening to each building.

Aerial photographs show the dope shop building having a brick chimney block attached to its southern elevation. The photographs also appear to show the building having asbestos sheeting for its roof and white rendered exterior walls which based on the foundations would have been constructed from single brick, concrete masonry units. Like many other buildings on the site, the concrete masonry units used during construction comprised a fly ash fill, with a cement rendered outer casing.

In addition to the dope shop recorded in the south west area of the site, an additional dope shop was located in a second technical area on the eastern area side of the aerodrome. We do not have a date to tell us if both technical areas were built at the same time, although with the arrival of two squadrons in the autumn of 1916 and each being designated their own operational sectors, it is suggestive that both are contemporaneous. It has not been possible to record the eastern technical area dope shop at the time of writing; the area of land was cleared down to foundation level and is now

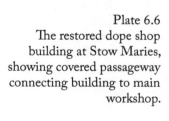

Plate 6.6
The restored dope shop
building at Stow Maries,
showing covered passageway
connecting building to main
workshop.

under dense woodland. Aerial photographs from September 1917 onwards (the earliest date for aerial photographs of the site) clearly show the dope shop located in a similar alignment in the eastern technical area to that on the western side.

Workshop

In 2012 surveying began on the building foundation directly to the north of the dope shop, in the western technical area. The building measured 29 feet in width and 144 feet in length, the dimensions matching those of one type of workshop listed on the post-war auction lists (two different sizes of workshops are listed for sale, both 29 feet in width but one type 144 feet in length and another 124 feet in length). A second workshop was later located in the eastern technical area, post-war clearing has made recording impractical but aerial photographs do show a workshop building (directly to the north of a dope shop, as per the western technical area) with matching dimensions.

The western technical area workshop was aligned north-south and divided into three individual units. The southern unit had an earth base, suggesting that the original timber suspended floor had been removed. The central and northern units of the building both had concrete flooring.

The southern section of the building contained a large double door entrance, which would have allowed a whole aircraft to pass through. A pathway made of bitumen-covered concrete beams leads from this doorway to the dope shop,

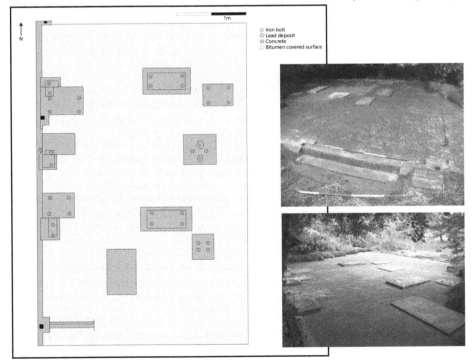

Fig. 6.4
Plan of workshop building recorded in the western technical area of the site.

Plates 6.7 and 6.8
Exposed floor area of main workshop building at Sedgeford, showing concrete plinths which were used as mounts for machinery.

suggesting that the southern unit of the workshop was the sailmaker's shop where repaired fabric for wings or sections of airframe were made and fitted before transferring to the dope shop for the fabric to be treated.

The central and northern units of the building appear to have been used as a carpenter's shop and a machine shop for repairing metal parts of the aircraft.

The floor contained a number of concrete machine bases, many with the original threaded studs for attaching machinery. Interestingly these concrete bases had undergone modification over time, new bases overlying older ones, with three successive layouts being observed. The machine shop contained a double doorway on its eastern elevation, with a gently sloping tarmac ramp leading to the roadway. The above has been deduced from working with the building's foundations which were partly incomplete. Official building plans for some workshop buildings show the dope shop, machine shop, carpenter's shop and sailmaker's shop all in a combined building. The layout of the workshops and dope shops at Sedgeford appear to have been designed to allow the various aircraft parts to be worked on and processed in sequence.

As with the dope shop, Stow Maries aerodrome also has a workshop building that has been completely refurbished. This building appears to be of similar dimensions and its layout offers a template to that of Sedgeford. The workshop comprised three units which were divided into fourteen bays. The southern and central units appear to have been of equal dimensions, with the northern unit being the larger of the three. Eleven windows appear on its side elevation which also contains three double-width wooden doors of equal size, with driveways connecting each door to the roadway of the technical area.

Motor Transport Shed

The aerodrome had two sets of Motor Transport (MT) sheds, which would have been used for storing vehicles used on the site. Each set of sheds comprises of two facing buildings. One set of MT sheds is located to the west of the Whin Close woodland, the other to the north of the eastern technical area. It is believed that both sets of MT sheds were built contemporaneously. The western MT area comprised two parallel sheds, aligned east-west. Each shed was divided into eight bays. Most of the bays were used for vehicle storage, with an office/storeroom at the eastern end and a three vehicle repair bay at the western end of the shed. Each of the facing elevations of the shed were un-enclosed, with both buildings separated from each other by a concrete square, measuring 100 feet by 55 feet. The eastern MT area was of similar design, except that its sheds were aligned north-south.

All bar one of the MT buildings were removed after the site became inactive. It appears that one set of buildings was quickly taken from the site, a second set still appears on an auction list dated 27th January, 1921. The foundations of the eastern area MT buildings are now under a densely wooded area, which also has been covered with a substantial amount of soil and rubble when part of the site was cleared several years ago. However, it has been possible to clearly locate the foundations of the western MT sheds and in 2015, this MT site was surveyed and recorded to see if it was possible to determine its layout. Accumulated debris and undergrowth had to be cleared back but it was possible to expose most of the foundations of the southernmost shed. The access to the sheds was constructed using a series of concrete bases into which timber supporting posts had been set. Dividing bases of concrete were then laid north-south, to form a series of bays. The rear and side walls were of timber construction. From aerial photographs, it appears that the northernmost MT shed had some of its bays at the eastern end converted to office space.

Recording of the building uncovered a series of concrete bases, measuring

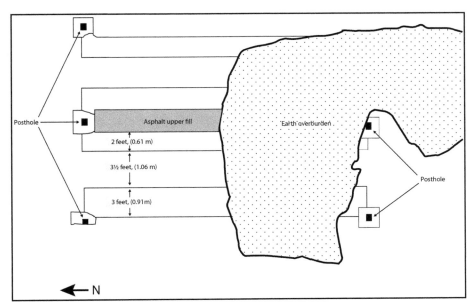

Fig. 6.5
Plan of recorded area of MT Shed in western technical area of site.

28 inches by 28 inches, used to support 4 inch x 4 inch timber posts. The concrete posthole bases were spaced 7 feet 6 inches apart and appear to have been the first phase of the building to be constructed. The timber posts would

have supported asbestos cement sheets to make up the building's walls, the roof of corrugated iron or asbestos sheets being supported by timber trusses. MT sheds found at other sites, such as Stow Maries and Marske, appear to have been built slightly later than that of Sedgeford, with brick walls and metal roof trusses being used in their construction. A series of

Plate 6.9
Exposed vehicle bays of MT Shed in western technical area of the site. The building in the upper left of the photograph is a contemporary farm building.

concrete dividing bases (using less aggregate than that used for the post hole bases) were then laid. The bases, measuring 2 feet across and spaced 3 feet 5 inches apart, allowed a vehicle such as a Crossley tender to be driven on to them. Each vehicle bay measured 11 feet in width and 12 feet in length. The ground between the concrete bases had been backfilled

Plate 6.10
Original Motor Transport shed at Stow Maries. The walls of the Sedgeford building were constructed using asbestos cement sheeting rather than brickwork as at later sites such as Stow Maries.

with rubble and it was not able to ascertain their depth or the type of material they originally contained.

Technical Store

One of the site's remaining standing buildings, the technical store, is situated on the western side of the woodland and forms part of a complex of buildings observed on aerial photographs as being the western Motor Transport (MT) technical area. The building was originally used as a technical store, serving the

MT sheds and other workshops on the site.

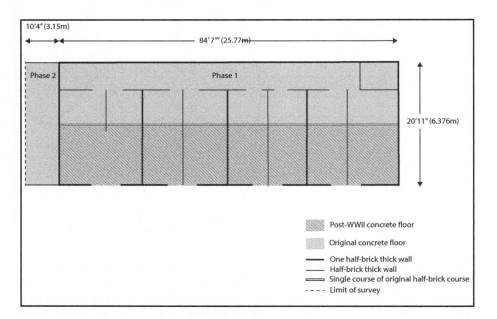

Fig. 6.6
Plan of Technical Store
building

Today the northern half of the building is in serious disrepair and appears unused since its original role. However, the southern half of the building is in relatively good order and shows signs of more recent redesign and usage as animal/bird stock pens. An electricity board inspection card on the fuse box being last updated on 26th June 1975.

A survey was carried out on the building in 2014 which showed that it had been constructed in three separate phases, extending the building in a northerly direction. All phases appeared contemporary with WWI building styles and materials and the suggestion is that the two extension phases were part of the significant expansion of the site during 1918. The original phase of the building was 80 feet 7 inches in length and 20 feet 11 inches wide.

Official technical store plans, dating to the latter part of 1917, show a building of similar design to that at Sedgeford. A significant difference is being a central double-door entrance on the official plans, whereas the technical store at Sedgeford appears to have multiple doors. The official plans also show an additional storage area at the rear of the main building, adjoined to a catslide roof and with double width doors at each elevation. This additional storage area appears to have been designated for the storage of metal and timber, along with packing cases. The technical store building at Sedgeford does not have this additional storage present.

Within the main technical store building, the area would have featured multiple sections of timber racking of varying sizes, along with timber pigeon holes for smaller items, a section for storing struts and a separate storage area for tyres. The building would also have had two internal offices. It has not been possible to locate the precise location of the offices on the Sedgeford building due to the subsequent renovation work outlined below.

As part of the original building's post-WW2 use as animal stock pens, a course concrete floor has been relaid which includes integral feeding trays and drainage sumps. The western half of the interior has been divided by single course brick walls into eight stock pens. The remains of an original course of bricks running north-south through the middle of the building suggests that it was originally divided into two areas. This suggests that larger items were being stored in the front section of the building with smaller items being held in the rear. The later extended phases suggest a possible administrative use to this new area. No access doorways are included in the newer sections and wooden framed service hatches were placed below each window frame. It has not been possible to directly ascertain the purpose of the hatches, although their positioning suggests they may have been used to service supply orders through.

The exterior walls for all phases of the building are of single brick thickness. While the original phase of the building does not have any windows present, the two extended phases both have steel framed windows with timber lintels and cast concrete sills in their western elevation. The primary phase

Plate 6.11
The Technical Store building at Sedgeford. The extended second phase of the building is on the left.

of the building still has many of its original timber roof trusses in place, although replacement trusses have been added at a later date. The original roof has been replaced (perhaps several times). As previously mentioned, the later extension phases of the building are today in a serious state of disrepair and it has not been possible to conduct close inspection. Apart from a railway sleeper screw, very few datable artefacts were found inside the building itself. Brickwork samples of the building dated to the early part of the 20th century, identifying the manufacturer as being the Peterborough based London Brick Company.

Royal Engineers' Workshop

Two Royal Engineers' Workshop were present on the site, located in each of the aerodrome's respective technical areas. On the western technical area, only limited evidence of the building's foundations remain and is now within an overgrown expanse of mature trees and bushes. The eastern technical area's workshop was completed cleared and no evidence of the building remains. However, aerial photographs, both oblique and vertical, clearly show both of the buildings present. In the western technical area, the workshop is aligned north-south, located directly to the north of the ambulance station. The eastern technical area's workshop is aligned east-west. Both workshops having dimensions of 80 feet by 30 feet. The photographs show cement rendered walls, with asbestos sheet roofs.

The workshops were used for the testing of aircraft engines during service or repair, designed with a large work area they were divided into bays, with the building featuring two outshots at either end of the which themselves contained further bays. The outshots formed a yard at the rear of the building. One of the oblique aerial photographs appears to show the yard of the western technical area workshop enclosed by wooden gates. There also appears to be

Fig. 6.7
Plan of Royal Engineers's
workshop recorded at
Sedgeford

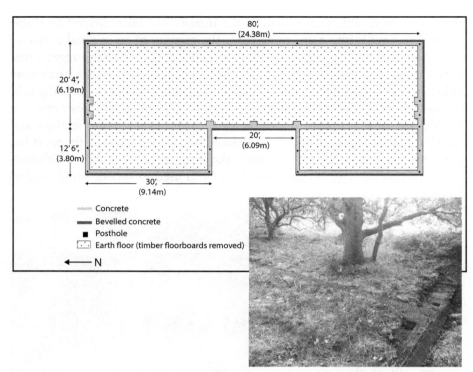

Plate 6.12
Foundations of the Royal
Engineers' workshop. The
tree in the centre of the
photograph is growing
within one of the outshots at
the rear of the building. The
remains of the the cement
rendered, concrete masonry
units used to construct the
building's wall can be seen
in the lower right of the
photograph.

double doors on the southern elevation of the outshot. Usually the bays within the workshops were divided up per squadron. At Sedgeford it appears that there was a dedicated workshop for each squadron.

Ambulance Station

The ambulance station at Sedgeford was located in the middle of the western technical area buildings. The technical area was served by a roadway, which offered direct access on to the landing ground itself or elsewhere on the site. No evidence for the building has been found during the recording process. From analysing aerial photographs, the building appears to have been 40 feet long by 15 wide and of timber framed construction.

Blacksmith

Located to the north of the Royal Engineers' workshop in the western technical area, the blacksmith building was yet another feature to leave only very ephemeral traces; with only its foundations remaining. The building appears on an oblique aerial photograph from 1918 and it appears to be very similar in design to that of the restored blacksmith building at Stow Maries. A courtyard with wooden access gates encloses the front of the building. Survey of the site revealed a series of concrete post holes around the courtyard. Unlike the blacksmith building at Stow Maries, which has a brick walled enclosure to its courtyard, Sedgeford's building appears to have had a fence supported by timber posts. The main building appears on aerial photographs to have had light coloured, cement rendered walls. The building's foundations show minimal traces of brickwork still affixed which suggest a similar concrete masonry units used to that found on the dope shop. The main blacksmith building measures 20 feet by 16 feet, aligned north-south, with a single window in the southern and western elevations. A chimney for the forge is located to the rear of the building.

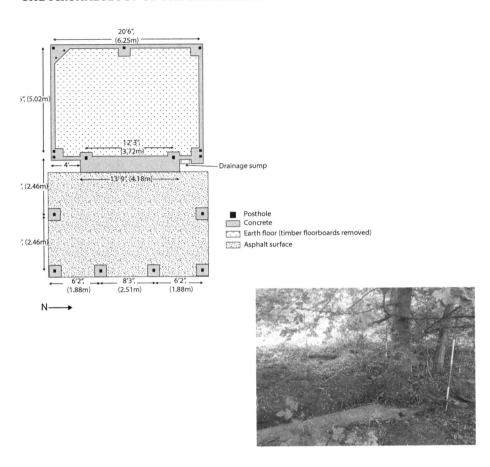

Fig. 6.8
Plan of blacksmith building.

Plate 6.13
The foundations of the site's blacksmith building. The ranging poles represent the postholes of the fence which enclosed the building's courtyard.

Coppersmith

This building has yet to be fully recorded but it appears on aerial photographs and site auction lists. The site of the coppersmith building has been fully cleared and little evidence remains today. Measurements taken from aerial photographs suggest dimensions of 30 feet by 15 feet, with cement rendered walls and external timber framing, and with two windows on the south elevation. There appears to be an enclosed yard to the rear of the building and behind that a small storage hut.

Machine Gun Range

The machine gun range, where airmen practised using the Lewis gun which they would later use in combat, was located in the north-eastern area of the site. The range itself comprised a levelled area, measuring 100 feet by 100 feet. The direction of fire was south to north with targets placed in front of a large earth bank, measuring 140 feet in length and 40 feet wide and approximately 10 feet high. A building appears on some aerial photographs, aligned directly along the range's eastern edge which may have been related to the range's use. Today it is still possible to discern the boundary of the range as an area set aside within the current agricultural field. During the clearing of the original aerodrome site, large pieces of concrete platform from the rail head, which ran close by, were pulled from the field to turn it back into agricultural use. The concrete was dumped on to the range and has subsequently become overgrown. Anecdotal evidence suggests that the range was in use during WWII by the local Home Guard unit, so it is possible that the major clearing of the site took place after WWII.

Fuel Store

Fuel stores of this period were fabricated in various sizes; 2,000, 4,000 and 6,000 gallons, with respective diameter dimensions of 9 feet 3 inches, 13 feet and 15 feet 9 inches. At Sedgeford, the fuel store was located at the southernmost end of the western technical area. At the time of writing this feature has yet to be recorded, although the overgrown area contains slabs of broken concrete and a protruding metal pipe.

It has not been possible to establish the exact size of the store that was located here. At other sites, fuel stores were usually constructed on a reinforced concrete base, with cement and brick buttressed 5 feet high walls. The circular tanks were built semi-underground, with the store covered by a reinforced concrete roof.

Generator (Power) Hut

Located in the south west corner of the site, immediately below G.S. Shed No. 3 and located within an area of trees and heavy undergrowth, are the foundation remains of what is believed to be a generator hut. The building is one of two identical structures; a further building has been identified (using aerial photographs) in a similar location within the eastern technical area of the site, suggesting that they would have performed similar functions for separate squadrons based at the aerodrome.

Plate 6.14
Floor of the generator hut building located in the site's western technical area.

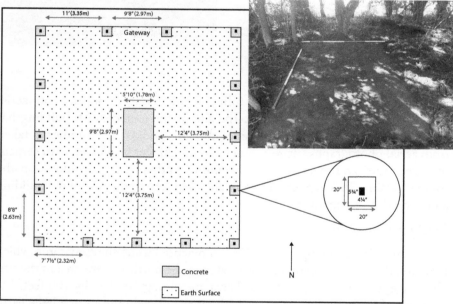

Fig. 6.9
Plan of generator hut recorded in western technical area.

The feature consists of a rectangular concrete floor, aligned north-south, which measures 9 feet 8 inches in length and 5 feet 6 inches wide. The floor was constructed of cement, sand and coarse aggregate on top of a hardcore surface aggregate and then a concrete beam foundation. Such a construction style gives the floor a total thickness of 10½ inches; a substantial thickness for such a small structure and one designed to carry a significant weight.

The concrete floor incorporated a recessed lip (4 inches) for the placement of wall panels, which would have been affixed by metal joints set into the concrete. The exterior edges of the floor surface also showed evidence of corrugated sheeting being used in the casting process.

Surrounding the floor surface were a series of concrete postholes. Aerial photographs show the building enclosed by a fence rather than a wall, giving the feature an enclosed area of 34 feet 6 inches in length by 30 feet 6 inches wide.

Official plans for on-site power houses constructed during that later phase of the war (such as that at Biggin Hill) suggest a larger building, which incorporated an engine/generator room, battery room, workshop/store and driver's room. The engine/generator room floor comprised two raised concrete beds for the engines. This later type of structure used 3 inch breeze concrete slabs which were toothed into brick piers every other course and then finished with an external wash of 75% cement and 25% Ironite.

Petrol Store

Described in the preceding section. Although it has not been possible to confirm if the petrol store was used during later phases of the site, the feature still appears in aerial photographs taken during 1917.

R.N.A.S. Flight Shed

As described in preceding section. It is believed that this building was still in active use during this phase and appears in several aerial photographs taken during 1917.

Flight Sheds

These are as described in preceding section and still in active use during this phase.

General Service (G.S.) Sheds

The G.S. shed was a new design of hangar introduced in 1916 which soon became a common feature on many British aerodromes and remained so through to the end of the war. A distinctive aspect of the hangar was its slightly curved roof, formed by the wooden trusses which incorporated intricate lattice work. The trusses were manufactured in Belfast and became known as Belfast Trusses (in some instances G.S. sheds are still referred to as Belfast Hangars).

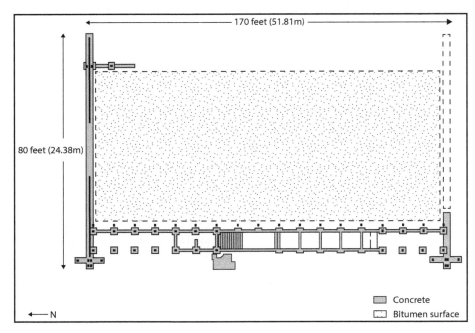

Fig. 6.10
Recorded plan of G.S. Shed No.1.

It has not been possible to confirm the actual construction dates of the three G.S. sheds that were constructed at Sedgeford. However, with the arrival of two full squadrons by autumn 1916, it is assumed that the hangars were in place by then. Two of the sheds (Sheds 1 and 2) were located along a north-south alignment on the eastern side (adjacent to the eastern technical area) of the Whin Close woodland. The remaining hangar (Shed 3) was also on a similar north-south alignment, but adjacent to the western technical area, located to the south of the twin flight sheds.

An aerial photograph of the site taken in 1946 shows that Shed 1 had already been removed by this date, but Sheds 2 and 3 are still standing (both were taken down shortly after this date). In 2010, SHARP began recording Sheds 1 and 2, using photographs and plans of the site to locate the features. With many areas of the aerodrome site having been reclaimed by nature over the preceding decades, the original location of the sheds required substantial clearing before the foundations were revealed.

Much of the work on Shed 1 was spent in revealing the western wall and both doors. The eastern side of the building was left unrecorded, having been covered by a heavy overburden of earth, along with having two Dutch barns being placed over it. Recording revealed an alignment of eighteen concrete postholes spaced ten feet apart along the western wall of the building. These postholes would have formed the hangar's western wall. A further alignment of postholes (although having one less posthole at its southern edge) was found further to the west of the building's main wall. Each of these postholes was spaced 11 feet 6 inches apart and were approximately 25 inches in depth and would have taken timber posts measuring 9 inches by 6 inches. The postholes contained evidence of metal bracing for each post. The surface of each posthole was cast in a concave fashion to dispel water from collecting against the wooden posts. The joists housed within the inner postholes would have comprised of three lengths of laminated timber which would have been bolted together to support the roof trusses. The outer alignment of postholes would have housed angled timber 'A' frame struts which would have given the building additional bracing. Later designs of the G.S. shed were to incorporate metal bracing frames. Each corner of Shed 1 showed signs of the concrete having cracked and undergone repair while in service.

Plate 6.15
The eastern wall foundation of G.S. Shed No.1. The doorway runner and gantry are visible at the bottom of the photograph. The foundations of the hangar's annexe can be seen towards the top.

At the northern and southern ends of the building, metal guides were inlaid into a concrete base indicating the doorways of the shed. A hangar would have had six timber framed doors at each end, clad with corrugated metal sheeting. At either end of the concrete door footings there were a further six postholes. This series of postholes extended slightly beyond those of the shed's bracing struts and would have been used for the timber framed door gantry. The door gantry at Sedgeford was of a similar design to that seen at Montrose air station. Later designs incorporated metal gantries and brick piers. The doors would have had a clear opening height of either 20 or 25 feet. Roofs for early phase G.S. sheds have been recorded as having been made of timber with felt cladding.

The foundations for an annexe, comprising of a series of rooms, were revealed along the western edge of Shed 1 and were located between the wall posts and the bracing struts. These rooms would have included an office, store rooms, dressing room and boiler room. One of the rooms also contained drainage pipes for a latrine. After excavation, several of the annexe's rooms appeared to have external doorsteps, while others only had access from within the hangar itself. The floors of the annexe rooms varied from bare earth, smooth concrete to rough cast concrete with regular grooves which appeared to be for the insertion of wooden flooring joists.

Survey work was also carried out on G.S. Shed No. 2. This building was located directly to the south of Shed 1 and was of similar layout and dimensions, the only variance being to some of the ancillary rooms in the annexe area. One of these rooms had a large concrete-lined pit that was one metre deep and had been divided into two cells. Shed 2 does appear on an early 1946 aerial photograph but later photographs from the same year show it to have been removed completely. The overall dimensions for the foundations of both Shed 1 and Shed 2 measured 170 feet (24.4m) x 80 feet (5.8m).

Plate 6.16
The south-facing doorway of G.S. Shed No.2.

G.S. Shed No. 3 was located in the south-west corner of the site, adjacent to the western technical area. This feature has yet been fully recorded. The site of the building is under a dense covering of undergrowth and trees, although this vegetation clearly delineates the profile of the original building. As in the case of Shed 2, aerial photographs taken in the early part of 1946 show Shed 3 still in place but later ones taken that year show it to have been removed.

Plate 6.17
South-facing door gantry foundation of G.S. Shed No.3.

Bessonneau Hangars

By September 1917, four Bessonneau hangars were in use on the site; this being a period just prior to when three squadrons were to be stationed on the site, requiring additional hangar space. An aerial photograph taken on 5th September of that year shows the vacant imprint of the original Bessonneau hangar used by the R.N.A.S. Four new Bessonneau hangars are in evidence on the eastern side of the site. All of these hangars are aligned north-south, with the opening to the east. It appears that the northernmost hangar has been erected first, then the adjacent space taken up by temporary canvas bell tents, with the next three hangars being placed together. Measurements taken from the photographs suggest the hangars measured 80 feet x 64 feet.

Storage Huts

Some of the storage huts from the R.N.A.S. phase of the site were still in evidence during 1917. Certainly more buildings were used for storage during this period but it has not been possible to locate these. accurately

Photographic Hut

This would have been a timber framed building located on the south east corner of the Whin Close woodland, used to develop film taken from aircraft and to also carry out photographic instruction. The photographic hut, measuring 18 feet x 15 feet, appears on aerial photographs (where it is specifically annotated) and also as anonymous building on the 1919 auction list. As a timber framed hut, it was likely to have had a foundation of modest brick piers. The hut itself would usually have been partitioned into five separate offices which carried out the production and administration functions. The rooms would have incorporated benches and sinks for the photographic development process, with shutters affixed to all windows. With this area having been under historic agricultural use no evidence remains. The building has not been recorded.

Wireless Hut

Located adjacent to the photographic hut, this was a smaller timber building which also appears on aerial photographs from 1917 (where it is specifically annotated) but no evidence of its foundation remains. Official plans show that this building was divided up into five smaller rooms and also sometimes being shared with the Bombing section. The building has not been recorded.

Instructional Huts

At least one instructional hut was located on the site. A timber framed building, measuring 80 feet x 15 feet and aligned east-west, to the north of the domestic area, adjacent to the northern perimeter of the roadway which circuits Whin Close. Again, this building was specifically annotated on the 4th September, 1917 aerial photograph. No evidence remains of the building today, with its location being under a section of dense undergrowth where the woodland has expanded.

Official building plans from the period outline different types of instructional huts used at other aerodromes, including a General Lecture Hut, which was divided into two rooms, one being the main lecture area and measuring 60 feet in length. The second type being the Gunnery Instruction Hut, which was divided into four rooms. Two larger rooms were used for lectures and two smaller rooms at either end of the building were used for instruction or as an armoury.

Squadron Office

The expansion of Sedgeford to a two squadron aerodrome required two separate squadron offices on the site. It appears that the first of these was located directly in front of some of the original R.N.A.S. buildings on the southern perimeter of Whin Close. An aerial photograph, dated September 1917, specifically identifies this building as being 64 Squadron's office. Approximated dimensions taken from the photograph suggest it as being 40 feet long x 20 feet wide. Subsequent development of this area saw a new squadron office building built during late 1918 (this building is still in place today) and as such no evidence remains of the original office.

A second squadron office was located adjacent to the northern perimeter roadway which circuits the woodland. In the same September 1917 aerial photograph, this building is identified as being 65 Training Squadron's office. The photograph shows this as being an identical building to that of 64 Squadron's office. The site of this building is now under substantial woodland and has not been recorded.

Mortuary

The mortuary building is located within the south west section of the Whin Close woodland. Then, as now, the dense trees and bushes would have concealed any building or structure placed here; indeed, the building does not appear on any of the aerial photographs taken of the aerodrome during WWI. In locating the mortuary, it appears as if considerable thought was taken in its placement; with a view to keeping it hidden away from the rest of the site. Unlike mortuary buildings found at other sites, such as Stow Maries, the building at Sedgeford does not incorporate an ambulance shed., the ambulance shed at Sedgeford being located within the western technical area of the site.

It has not been able to obtain an exact date for the mortuary's construction. However, the development of the aerodrome and attritional nature of its training suggests that a mortuary building would unfortunately have to have been an early requirement. There may originally have been a previous structure made from more temporary materials but the building that still remains today does match one that appears on a site auction list, dated 27th January 1921.

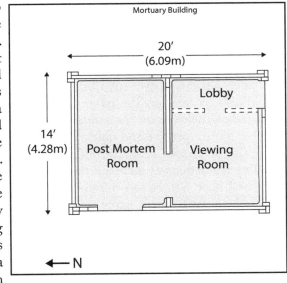

Fig. 6.11
Plan of mortuary building

The mortuary building at Sedgeford's has overall dimensions of 20 feet x 14 feet, and was originally divided into three separate rooms. The northernmost room was the post mortem room, measuring 10 feet in width, and was entranced by a double-width doorway which would have enabled access for a stretcher. The adjoining room was partitioned into two areas. The lobby was accessed by a single-width external door. The partitioning wall, which separates the lobby from the larger viewing room, has been removed post-service use at some point. The post mortem room has four adjustable air vents set into its wall, two at ground level and two at ceiling height. The room also has a cement skim at the base of the walls, forming a curve against the floor which would have enabled easier cleaning.

Although part of the slate tile roof has collapsed, enough remains to show a louvered wooden frame on the top centre of the roof which would have enabled ventilation. This particular means of ventilation has been found on other mortuary buildings from the late Victorian period. All of the mortuary building's windows are placed towards the top of the walls. It would not have been possible for someone outside of the building to look into the interior but the windows still allowed natural light to enter.

Plate 6.18
The mortuary building at Sedgeford. The hollow clay bricks used to construct the walls of the building can clearly be seen.

A distinguishing visual feature of the building is its brickwork. The building is built on a concrete foundation which incorporates a ground course of bricks made by the Whittlesey Central Brick Company, near Peterborough. Similar bricks are used on the columns at each corner of the building. However, of most interest are the bricks used for the exterior and interior walls. Rather than conventional bricks, these are hollow clay bricks. Initially it was believed that the hollow bricks would have offered assistance in keeping the building at an ambient temperature but our research seems to point towards their use in this building as being more utilitarian. Hollow clay bricks were largely used during this period for interior walls, before the advent of concrete blocks. The hollow bricks would not have been used to offer any significant thermal insulation advantage over solid brick and their durability against weathering would also be inferior. The latter point is exemplified by their deteriorated state today. Their use on the mortuary building at Sedgeford points towards it being an inexpensive and quicker alternative than conventional brickwork. Interestingly Crown Properties of this period did not have to comply with building regulations as such and the type of brickwork used on the mortuary may well have not passed minimum thickness regulations. The mortuary's hollow brickwork shows many signs of having been repaired with a cement fill. It has not been possible to apply a date as to when this repair took place but as no other accounts exist for the buildings later use, it is assumed that this restoration took place during the building's original period of use.

Regrettably, the mortuary building at Sedgeford Aerodrome would have seen frequent use over its period of operation. Its concealed location ensured that the daily risk posed by flying, which too often resulted in fatalities, was kept as far away from general view as possible.

Compass Platform

The compass platform comprised a concrete circle cast into the ground which was used to calibrate an aircraft's compass for any heading deviation. The aircraft would be turned 360° around the platform and the aircraft compass assessed against a master compass. The compass platform at Sedgeford was located on the southern perimeter of Whin Close and measured approximately 35 feet in diameter. The platform appears on the 1917 aerial photograph but evidence was lost when this area of the site was returned back to agricultural use. A magnetometer survey of the area during November 2016 highlighted the original foundation of this feature.

Landing Circle

This feature was a chalk marked circle, measuring 150 feet in diameter, located towards the western edge of the landing ground.

Landing Ground

The landing ground was located within the south east area of the main site and aligned east-west. The area's boundary was marked out in chalk, including vertical line markings running across the field at 75 feet intervals. Although the site itself is positioned on the ridge of the Heacham River valley (at a height of 58m above sea level), the landing ground is extremely flat and has no lateral obstacles on the flight path. However, Whin Close and adjacent woodland down the valley would require attention. The geology of the site would have been excellently suited for an aerodrome, an area of chalk upland which gradually descends to a river valley, allowing perfect drainage.

The Regimental Buildings

Canteen

Located at the northern end of the site, the canteen was yet another timber framed building, listed on the 12th June, 1919 auction list as having dimensions of 120 feet x 15 feet. The canteen was aligned east-west and was in close proximity to the main barracks area. An oblique aerial photograph shows a series of smaller wooden huts located to the rear of the building. The light foundations of all of these buildings are now hidden under dense undergrowth of the expanded woodland. The building has not been recorded.

Accommodation Buildings

The main group of accommodation buildings were located in the north west area of the site. Six timber framed buildings have been identified from aerial photographs (there may be more than this but it has not been possible to identify all buildings at the time of writing). It has not been possible to record the site of the buildings but two auction lists give their measurements; three being 100 feet x 15 feet and two being 106 feet x 34 feet. Accommodation buildings built on other sites at a later date during the war are of brick construction with slate roofs. The Sedgeford buildings were of a very basic design, with only a single stove for heating. Aerial photographs taken during 1917 still show the original R.N.A.S. building in place and due to the premium on accommodation spaces at Sedgeford, it is entirely possible that this building would also have been used for accommodation.

Temporary Camping Areas

In the 4th September 1917 aerial photograph, almost fifty white canvas bell tents can be identified. Most of these were located in defined groupings on the north east side of the site, although some tents can be seen to intermingle around other buildings such as the Bessonneau hangars. During this period, the main accommodation buildings were under extreme pressure and unable to cope with the influx of new arrivals to the site. The photographs taken during 1917 do not appear to show any ongoing development or construction and it is assumed that the tents would have been used during the winter months.

Officers' Quarters and Billets

From 1916 onwards, many officers stationed at Sedgeford were billeted at the Old Docking Workhouse (now Norfolk Heights) and shuttled to and from the aerodrome. Records suggest that others were billeted in the village of Sedgeford as well. It has not been possible to identify any dedicated officers' quarters on the site itself during this phase.

Regimental Institute

The Regimental Institute was located close to the northern boundary of the site, adjacent to the main roadway on to the site itself. The building appears on the 27th January, 1921 auction list as having dimensions of 100 feet x 99 feet. The institute does not appear clearly on any aerial photographs. Anecdotal records refer to the building being sold at auction and moved to Heacham. This area of the site has been under agricultural use since the site closed after WWI. No evidence remains of the building's foundations.

Guard House

Located next to the regimental institute, the guard house was also a timber framed building, its dimensions being 80 feet x 30 feet and aligned north-south. The building was accessed from the main roadway to the site by a semicircular driveway. Examples of guard houses from other sites, such as Marske, make comparison difficult as they appear to be of later, brick construction. Official building plans for the guard house show it comprising of a veranda across its front elevation and two main rooms within the building itself; a guard room and a detention room. An enclosed yard was located to the rear of the building.

Unidentified Buildings

A significant number of buildings appear on aerial photographs and in documentary records, at the time of writing, have not been possible to positively identify. There are still several buildings that are 'missing' from this phase of the site; specifically domestic buildings such as latrines, baths and mess huts. Some of the technical buildings which should be present also await discovery.

Phase 3 (1918)

By the summer of 1918, the aerodrome had seen substantial expansion from its humble origins. Some of the original buildings were still in place and in active use but during this later phase we see a significant increase in the number of accommodation buildings (along with large temporary accommodation areas as well). It appears that the technical buildings that served the aerodrome in its earlier phases are largely the same in number. Since late 1917, the base has been contemporaneously home to three squadrons. Although some of these numbers were lighter at the turn of the year, by summer 1918 large numbers of personnel have arrived on site.

From aerial photographs taken during 1918, along with documentary accounts from the period, it appears that the site was struggling to house all of its new arrivals; with numerous temporary camping areas of white canvas bell tents appearing around the site. A site status memorandum, produced

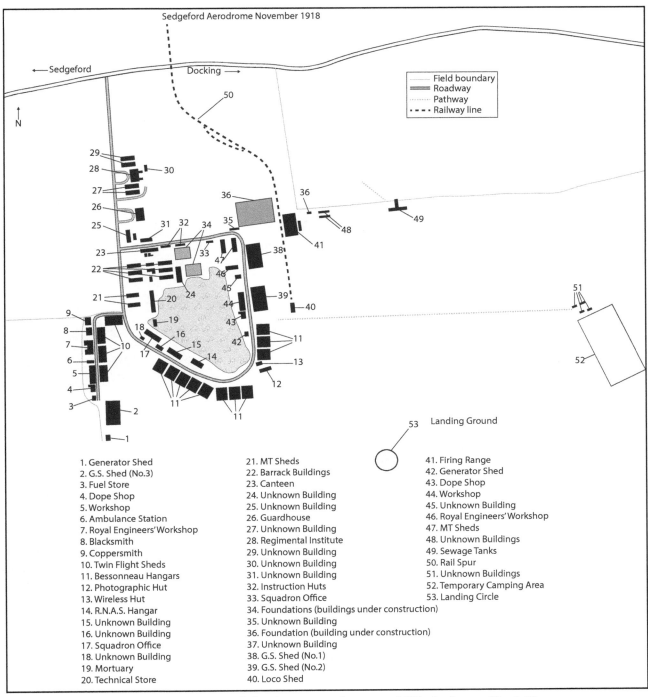

Sedgeford Aerodrome November 1918

← Sedgeford   Docking →

	Field boundary
	Roadway
	Pathway
	Railway line

N

1. Generator Shed
2. G.S. Shed (No.3)
3. Fuel Store
4. Dope Shop
5. Workshop
6. Ambulance Station
7. Royal Engineers' Workshop
8. Blacksmith
9. Coppersmith
10. Twin Flight Sheds
11. Bessonneau Hangars
12. Photographic Hut
13. Wireless Hut
14. R.N.A.S. Hangar
15. Unknown Building
16. Unknown Building
17. Squadron Office
18. Unknown Building
19. Mortuary
20. Technical Store

21. MT Sheds
22. Barrack Buildings
23. Canteen
24. Unknown Building
25. Unknown Building
26. Guardhouse
27. Unknown Building
28. Regimental Institute
29. Unknown Building
30. Unknown Building
31. Unknown Building
32. Instruction Huts
33. Squadron Office
34. Foundations (buildings under construction)
35. Unknown Building
36. Foundation (building under construction)
37. Unknown Building
38. G.S. Shed (No.1)
39. G.S. Shed (No.2)
40. Loco Shed

41. Firing Range
42. Generator Shed
43. Dope Shop
44. Workshop
45. Unknown Building
46. Royal Engineers' Workshop
47. MT Sheds
48. Unknown Buildings
49. Sewage Tanks
50. Rail Spur
51. Unknown Buildings
52. Temporary Camping Area
53. Landing Circle

53 Landing Ground

in October 1918 by No. 3 Fighting School, reports that two MT sheds (presumably those located in the eastern technical area) and the old Naval hangar were in the process of being converted into sleeping quarters, with refurbishment 75% complete as of the 15th October, 1918. It also appears that new hangars were in the process of being constructed during late 1918, with up to eleven Bessonneau hangars being used on a temporary basis.

Not only do we witness a sizeable increase in the number of buildings being constructed on the site, it appears that these new buildings are being built to a much more permanent design. A railway spur is laid, connecting the

Fig. 6.12
Site plan of Sedgeford aerodrome, showing buildings and features present during its expansion period in November 1918.

Plate 6.19
Near vertical aerial
photograph taken of the
Sedgeford site on 5th
November, 1918. The railway
spur, connecting the site to
the Heacham-Wells railway
can be seen snaking across
the field in the upper left
part of the photograph. The
white buildings aligned
around the Whin Close
woodland are temporary
Bessonneau hangars. A
temporary camping area for
new personnel can be seen
in the upper right of the
photograph.

site to the nearby Heacham to Wells Great Eastern Railways (G.E.R.) line. New brick built accommodation buildings and a coupled G.S. shed were in the process of construction. The aerodrome even had its own cinema building.

The picture of the aerodrome during the summer and autumn months of 1918 was one of intense activity and development in order to bring Sedgeford up to full status as a three unit training depot. Then, just as the new buildings were on the point of completion, the news of the Armistice broke and development came to a halt.

The Technical Buildings

Dope Shop

Described in preceding section.

Workshops

Described in preceding section.

MT Sheds

As described in the preceding section, although a communique written by No. 3 Fighting School prior to its arrival at Sedgeford during November 1918 notes that two of the MT sheds are in the process of conversion into accommodation blocks. It is assumed that this refers to the MT sheds in the eastern technical area. The conversion to accommodation is 75% complete as of 15th October, 1918.

Technical Store

Described in preceding section.

Royal Engineers' Workshop

Described in preceding section.

Ambulance Station

Described in preceding section.

Unidentified Building

By July 1918 a new building had been built directly to the north of the ambulance station. Several aerial photos show this to be building approximately 8 feet in width and 30 feet in length. Its positioning, directly adjacent to the ambulance station, suggests some form of relationship. Little information can be discerned from the photographs, except that it appears to be built using dark brick. The rear elevation contains a small window and there appears to be a brick built chimney on its roof. The building has yet to be recorded.

Blacksmith

Described in preceding section.

Coppersmith

Described in preceding section.

Machine Gun Range

Described in preceding section.

Fuel Store

Described in preceding section.

R.N.A.S. Flight Shed

The R.N.A.S. flight shed is still in its original position during this phase, although by the autumn it is being converted into sleeping quarters. The No. 3 Fighting School memorandum, dated 15th October, states work as being 75% completed.

Twin Flight Sheds

As described in preceding section.

General Service (G.S.) Sheds

All three of the original G.S. sheds (see preceding section) are still in active use throughout 1918. However, aerial photographs taken during July 1918 show significant construction ongoing in the north east area of the site, with a large rectangular-shaped area of land having been cleared. By early November, the building under construction appears to have hardly progressed except for what appear to be three north-south aligned foundation trenches, (approximately 10 feet in width), each equally spaced apart and which subdivide the main plot into two uniform areas. Taking measurements from the aerial photographs, the entire building plot measures 190 feet in length and 210 feet wide. Taking the interior measurements of the subdivided areas gives approximate measurements of 100 feet wide and 180 feet in length. The suggestion from these measurements and the type of foundations being used, was that the building under construction was to be a coupled G.S. shed, perhaps similar in design to that at nearby Bircham Newton. In the event, the aerial photograph taken on the 5th November, 1918 shows how far the construction reached, with the Armistice being signed the following week and work halting shortly after.

Bessonneau Hangars

During the summer of 1918, at least three Bessonneau hangars arrive on site and are located around the south eastern perimeter of the Whin Close woodland. It is possible that the hangars may have arrived earlier in the year, when the aerodrome was host to three squadrons, although no records are available to confirm this. We do know that by the beginning of November, the number of Bessonneau hangars had increased to eleven. Three were located directly below G.S. Shed No. 2, another three immediately south of Whin Close, joined by a further five facing a south-westerly direction. All hangars appear to be of the six bay type, measuring 80 feet x 64 feet. The expansion in the number of these hangars may coincide with the conversion of some of the G.S. sheds over to accommodation use.

Storage Huts

Described in preceding section.

Photographic Hut

Described in preceding section.

Wireless Hut

Described in preceding section.

Instructional Huts

By 1918, two instructional huts are identified within the northern area of the site. Both appear to be timber framed buildings, aligned east-west and measuring approximately 80 feet in length by 15 feet in width. It is highly likely that other instructional huts were also in use during this period but it has not been possible to identify them.

Squadron Office

The two squadron offices described in the preceding section appear to still be in operation during this phase. It is likely that a third office may also in use from the beginning of 1918, although this building has yet to be identified.

However we do know that very late in the site's development, a new brick built squadron office is constructed along the south-eastern perimeter of the Whin Close woodland. This new building appears to have been built directly over the original squadron office in the same location. It has not been possible to obtain an actual date for this building's construction. The building does not appear on an aerial photograph taken on 4th November, 1918, although anecdotal accounts place it on the site at the beginning of 1919.

The building appears to have been used as accommodation for personnel stationed on the daytime decoy (K) site during WWII . During this period the shelter, directly to the north of the building, was constructed along with a separate latrine building and sewage system also being added. Following WWII, the original building appears to have been converted into three separate residential dwellings,

Plate 6.20
The squadron office building at the southern edge of Whin Close. The buildings were converted to domestic dwellings after WWII.

each having a separate toilet/washroom annexe added to the main building. Anecdotal records suggest that the building was still in use during the late 1960s to early 1970s as residential dwellings. At some point following, the building was then converted into stockholding pens for game birds.

Mortuary

Described in preceding section.

Compass Platform

From aerial photographs taken from the summer onwards, the compass platform is not visible in its previous location, as it has been covered by a Bessonneau hangar. It does not appear to have been relocated.

Landing Circle

Described in preceding section.

Landing Ground

Described in preceding section.

Railway Spur

A significant addition to the site occurred during late 1918 with the installation of a railway spur, linking the aerodrome site to the Heacham to Wells, Great Eastern Railways (G.E.R.) line. Until the introduction of its own spur, the aerodrome had been collecting most of its supplies from nearby Docking station. However, the expansion of the site would require the transportation of significant quantities of building materials, along with the additional supplies and provisions to cater for the increased number of personnel.

Oblique aerial photographs taken on 31st July, 1918, show the aerodrome with some of the construction work underway; the coupled G.S. shed has its foundations being prepared. Several temporary camping areas can also been seen within the same field (adjacent to the Sedgeford-Docking road) but no sign of a railway line is observable. On a vertical aerial photograph, taken on 5th November, the railway line can be clearly seen, snaking diagonally across the field. The same photograph also shows substantial quantities of materials already having been offloaded along the track in the middle of the field.

The railway spur branched from the main Heacham to Wells line (a standard gauge track of 4 feet 8 1/2 inches) and followed a field boundary in a southerly direction towards the B1454 Sedgeford to Docking Road. It is believed that the initial attempt at laying the track had to be aborted due to problems encountered with the underlying geology on this initial stage. The spur, measuring approximately half a mile in length, was quickly completed and according to a local resident whose grandfather was a guard on the G.E.R. line, carriages were initially pulled along the spur to the aerodrome by horse. No plans or records exist for the railway line's assembly or its operation. The aerial photographs reveal no evidence of a locomotive or freight carriages or of a building which would have housed the locomotive. We do have confirmation that a locomotive shed was built at the railhead (a loco shed being listed on a later auction list and the building is featured on a hand drawn map of the aerodrome, made during the latter months of 1918).

Several other aerodromes from this period also appear to have had a light railway line laid to serve the site. During the construction of the aerodrome at Eastburn in West Yorkshire, the private contractors building the aerodrome laid a 24-inch narrow gauge line to serve the site's technical area. A well-tank 0-4-0 steam locomotive was used at Eastburn to move freight. Once the construction work was completed, the contractor was required to leave the railway and locomotive in place.

It does appears that Sedgeford's railway line was a very short-lived operation. Only active for a matter of months before closing down as construction at the site came to an end. Holcombe Ingleby describes the railway line's disappearance in his book *The Charm Of A Village* 'the railway lines that had been laid across the Docking Road were removed almost before they came into use'. Today the only trace to be seen of the original railway line is a slight undulation of the contemporary road surface and a gap that remains in the hedgerow where the track ran across the field towards the aerodrome.

Railhead

The railhead was the terminus for the rail spur and it appears to have been located directly to the east of G.S. Shed No. 2. In 2011, SHARP excavated this area to see if evidence could be found of the original rail line. Excavations revealed several concrete foundations that were aligned with the direction of the railway track. The foundations didn't suggest an enclosed building, such as a locomotive shed but may have been used as support structures for a water tower (another building included on later site auction lists). A large amount of brickwork and concrete were removed from the field after WWII, after it underwent mechanised ploughing. It is likely that these concrete features would have been part of the goods platform, built to offload materials and supplies. Many discarded sections of the original concrete can still be found in the south east corner of the field where the railway crossed.

Locomotive Shed

No evidence has been found of the locomotive shed, presumed to have been located at the railhead. The building does not appear on the 5th November, 1918 aerial photograph. A locomotive shed is described on the 27th January 1921 auction list, which states its dimensions as being 30 feet x 15 feet (this listing also includes wooden water structures for sale with building). The auction list does not state the type of material it was built from, although a similar locomotive shed at Hendon aerodrome was of brick construction with two wooden entrance doors and a catslide roof over a room at the rear of the building. Based on the building styles adapted for other buildings being built on the site at this time, it is assumed that the locomotive shed would also have been of brick construction.

Bomb Dropping Tower

A feature has been identified on various aerial photographs, located along the south-east perimeter of the Whin Close woodland, which resembles a bomb dropping training tower. This feature is now within dense woodland and as yet has not been recorded.

The Regimental Buildings

Canteen

Described in preceding section.

Accommodation Buildings

Described in the preceding section. However, additional buildings appear on aerial photographs which match the dimensions of barrack blocks listed on the 27th January, 1921 auction list. Two sets of two buildings are located either side of the regimental institute building. The timber framed buildings measure approximately 106 feet in length x 34 feet in width and are aligned east-west. The location of these buildings, to the north and beyond the boundary of the guard house, are of interest. It raises the question as to whether these buildings were used to house the civilian workers employed at the site. These new buildings appear in an aerial photograph, dated 30th July, 1918, showing temporary tents arranged nearby. In a later aerial photograph taken in November, the buildings appear to be in full use, with the bare patches of the recently vacated tents clearly visible in the nearby field.

A women's hostel was located within the aerodrome's domestic area. A letter written by a Fiona May, dated 4th March, 1919, while she was serving in the W.R.A.F. with No.3 Fighting School at Sedgeford, gives greater insight into the women's accommodation area:

> … Now we are settled in to the huts I will tell you about them, there are nine:
> - kitchen
> - common room (not yet completed)
> - officers'
> - washing place etc.
> - household hut
> - clerks
> - transport hut
> - vacant at present
> - vacant at present
> - vacant at present

She describes sharing the transport hut, which was her allocated accommodation, with six others. Each having their own locker and washbasin.

Blankets were hung from the roof beams to afford them some privacy. A single stove heated the entire hut.

Temporary Camping Areas

Throughout 1918, the aerial photographs show numerous white canvas bell tents arranged around the site. In the early part of the year, many of them are pitched in the field that lies to the north of the aerodrome. Later in the year, as development and construction takes place within this field (including the laying of the rail spur), this temporary camping area is moved to another part of the site. By the 5th November, 1918 a dedicated camping area, containing approximately 50 tents, can clearly be identified at the very eastern boundary of the site. This temporary camping area appears to have a small number of timber framed buildings associated with it, probably latrines or washhouses.

Officers' Quarters and Billets

Described in preceding section.

Regimental Institute

Described in preceding section.

Guard House

Described in preceding section.

Cinema

Anecdotal accounts, along with a hand drawn map of the aerodrome, point to there being a cinema on the site. Based on other buildings included on the map, the cinema appears to have been built during the summer/autumn of 1918. It was located close to the locomotive shed at the end of the rail spur. The cinema appears to have been open for local villagers to attend screenings. Some accounts have the building featuring raked seating. This building has not been identified or recorded.

Foundations of Building Under Construction

Amongst the ongoing development on the aerodrome during 1918, two buildings under the early stages of construction are of particular interest. Located to the east of the domestic area, two sets of large open groundworks, measuring approximately 100 feet x 100 feet, can be discerned on an aerial photograph taken in early November. It is not possible to ascertain too much information from the photograph, except both of the features appear to have substantial concrete and brick foundations. Both are closely located to the domestic area. Perhaps more substantial, long-term accommodation buildings are being constructed? Certainly there was still pressure to move large numbers of personnel from their temporary accommodation into something more permanent. The buildings were not completed and their sites are now under thick undergrowth and woodland and have yet to be located and recorded.

Latrines

An aerodrome the size of Sedgeford would have required numerous latrine blocks. To date, none of these buildings have been recorded. A possible location for one such building has been identified from an aerial photograph as being to the east of the main site. Situated against a field boundary, two timber framed buildings; one measuring 120 feet in length and 20 feet in width and aligned east-west, the other measuring 60 feet in length and 15 feet in width but aligned north-south, have been conjoined into a T-shaped formation. From these buildings a trench/pipe runs diagonally across the adjoining field for around 225 feet. At the base of the trench/pipe there appears to be a feature resembling sewage tanks. This group of features has not been recorded.

Fire Hydrant

During recording in 2012, field surveying uncovered a metal fire hydrant cover amidst the now overgrown eastern technical area. The metal hydrant cover was made by Ham Baker & Co. of Westminster and plotting of the hydrant placed it directly to the left hand side of the entrance to G.S. Shed No.3. An identical cover was found during field survey, carried out in November, 2016, within an area located close to the original landing circle; suggesting that this cover had been discarded or moved by ploughing.

Unidentified Buildings

Large numbers of buildings, appearing on aerial photographs taken throughout 1918, have yet to be identified. Evaluating the buildings listed on various site auction lists, numerous buildings and features were in use on the aerodrome but still remain unidentified. These include: drying room, bath house, incinerator and storage huts.

The main accommodation area for NCOs and women was to the north of the site. Today this area is a field which has been under agricultural use for much of the post-war period. Many of the buildings used in the accommodation area were timber framed and left little evidence after removal. This area was densely populated and during much of 1918, many of the personnel were living in tents.

Auction Lists

After the Armistice, the development of the aerodrome, which up until that point in time had been moving at a rapid pace throughout the summer and autumn months, slowed significantly. No. 3 Fighting School was operating at half-strength by the turn of the year and after being re-designated No. 1 Training Squadron in March, 1919, it was finally disbanded in October of that year. The war years had put an incredible strain on the country's material resources and Sedgeford, like many other military establishments, became the focus of how to release valuable material back into the public domain in order to get the country moving forward.

Inventories were drawn up and on behalf of the Controller of the Disposal Board, with the auctioneers Miles & Son arranging an auction for Thursday, 12th June, 1919; the first of three such auctions to take place at Sedgeford. In fact the first sale was run while three groups were still operational at the aerodrome. The items to appear on the first auction list included:

44 army huts, buildings and shelters (mostly sectional), including:
1 x canteen - 120' x 15'
2 x sleeping huts - 100' x 15'
1 x hut - 80' x 15'
16 x huts - 60' x 15'

Range of well-built offices - 67' x 16'
Other structures, sizes varying to 8' x 6'

Huts and buildings in excellent condition with 4' x 2' framing rabbited F.El boarding outside with rubberoid roofs and lined with Uralite. The doors and windows are well made and the huts are capable of being admirably adapted for motor garages and houses, bungalows, offices, workshops, farm shelters etc. The corrugated iron structures are all painted in sound condition, as good as new.

Builders' and contractors' plant, including:

Smithy and blacksmith's appliances
3 & 6 ton chain blocks
6 sets of Sheave pulleys
Ladders
Navvies' shovels
Picks
Rammers
Hods
Mortar mixing boards
Galvanised tanks
Putlogs
Harrows
Buckets
Oil sheets
3 x 60' lengths of 1" rubber hose pipe
Stocks and die
Portable forge (by Alldays and Onions)
Anvils and blocks
Swage block and tools
Drilling and screwing machines
Vices
Tube cutter and two expanders
New 7lb and 10lb hammers
4 x 5 ton lifting jacks
Steam gauge
Floor cramps
Rail gauges and adxe hammers
4 x 200' lengths of new hemp rope
Quantity of new wire rope and fencing wire
Two diaphragm pumps on barrows complete with 20' lengths of hose
      pipe
Quantity of duplex hanging and wall lamps
Hurricane and danger lamps
Wood tank
20' x 6' x 5' 60 sheets of corrugated iron
Paint brushes
Kettles
Office furniture
249 x 2', 6" iron spring bedsteads, wool mattresses and pillows with
      Holland covers (nearly new)

On Thursday 27th January, 1921, a further auction was carried out by Ingram Watson & Son, with items for sale listed as:

> 3 x large flight sheds - 170' x 80'
> 2 x large buildings - 102' x 30'
> 2 x transport sheds - 95' x 30'
> 3 x buildings - guard house, drying room and bath house
> 1 x regimental institute - 100' x 99'
> 2 x blocks of workshops - 124' x 29' and 144' x 29'
> 8 x buildings of technical stores - 81' x 21' (Blacksmiths' shops, power station, ammunition and bomb stores and depot office, 84' x 30')
> 3 x barrack blocks (106' x 34')
> 1 x loco shed (30' x 15') and wood water structures
> 9 x erections of uncovered enclosures, huts, steel framework for hangars, observatory and meteorological office.
> 1 x incinerator
> 1 x latrines
> 1 x E.C.
> 1 x mortuary
> 1 x machine gun range

A third auction was carried out by Miles & Son on Wednesday and Thursday, 2nd and 3rd of February, 1921. Here the items included:

> 151 buildings - brick-built, wood and corrugated iron, standing thereon, comprising:
> 66 wooden sectional huts, with felt roofs, asbestos lining and wood floors - 8 flight sheds, 6 transport motor sheds, officers' and men's living and sleeping quarters, lecture and instructional huts, workshops, power houses, offices, regimental institute, W.A.A.C. hostel, barrack block.
> In addition, an iron water tank (8,000 gallons), electric light wiring and fittings throughout camp.
> About 400 lots of loose materials - boilers, hot water radiators and piping, portable farm boilers, slow combustion stoves, enamelled baths, w.c's, fittings, fire extinguishers and bucket, technical store lockers and pigeon holes, carpenter's benches and vices, office furniture, iron horse roll, portable crane, scrap iron and numerous other effects.

The auction lists give some indication of the huge operational undertaking which was required to run an aerodrome of the size of Sedgeford. During its peak capacity, just over 1,200 personnel were based there and the infrastructure, along with the day to day operational resources, would have been of a significantly higher level than that of the local communities.

Buildings in the Local Area

It appears that the auctions were successful. Many of the items listed for sale were quickly removed from the site. Unfortunately, no records exist which to tell us where the items ended up. However, with a keen eye it has been possible to trace some of the original buildings and several of these have not moved far at all.

Plate 6.21
One of Sedgeford's original
timber-framed flight sheds,
still in use today as a garage
in the nearby village of
Heacham.

The first feature to attract attention was at a garage in nearby Heacham, owned by John Beeken. While giving a lecture to a local historical society, an audience member recalled how his father had dismantled some of the original buildings and transported one to the sea front at Heacham. A conversation with John confirmed that his own father had indeed bought the building in question and relocated it to its current site. The exterior had always suggested itself as a possibility for an original Sedgeford building, Closer examination of the interior and the recording of its dimensions, suggested that it was one of the original flight sheds. The front elevation of the building has undergone significant modification over the years but the original timber cladding above the doors is still in place. The original roof has been replaced, although the roof trusses and exterior side walls and window frames appear to be of primary materials. One side of the interior has a half-partioned, original wall running along most of the building's length. The rear of the building, including roof, has fallen into disrepair.

Plate 6.22
Old postcard of domed-
roof building at North
Beach, Heacham. The roof
was purchased at auction
as a Nissen hut from the
Sedgeford site post-WWI.

Further buildings were also revealed in Heacham thanks to the discovery of a postcard, dated 9th August, 1932. The postcard shows a row of beach front cottages along Heacham's North Beach. It was the cottage in the foreground which raised the most curiosity. In the postcard the cottage is seen with a timber cladded walls on its ground floor, along with a covered veranda. However the second floor comprises an intriguing curved, corrugated iron roof. The roof appeared very similar in shape to that of the Nissen huts that were a feature of the Sedgeford aerodrome. It appears that the ground floor of the cottage was of conventional construction with the Nissen hut then affixed on top to become the upper floor. Today there are six such cottages along the front of North Beach, Heacham, all of which have a contemporary pitched roof concealing a curved inner ceiling.

Plate 6.23
North Beach, Heacham buildings today with pitched roof built over the original domed building.

A further anecdotal account, suggests that a building which may have been the original regimental institute at the aerodrome, was moved to a site on the beach side of the old railway station in Heacham. Redevelopment of this site several years ago removed all evidence of the this building.

The Material Culture

Much of the research undertaken on the aerodrome site has involved the surveying and recording of its key features. Very limited invasive excavation has been carried out, as such most of the finds discovered have been found in relatively high stratigraphic contexts. Many areas of the site have been intensively cleared, particularly during the post-WWII period, as such the location of some finds cannot always be relied upon for original deposition. Other areas of the site have now been under extensive agricultural use for almost a century, which also has the effect of re-deposition.

The finds themselves can largely be ordered into four main categories - glassware, ceramics, metal and leather/textiles.

Glassware

Of the 108 sherds of glassware recovered from the site, the majority have been found to the rear of the WWI squadron office (at the southern edge of the Whin Close woodland) in what appears to be a refuse deposit. It has only been possible to date about half of the sherds found due to their fragmented condition. This analysis has shown that almost 50% of the datable sherds were from vessels or objects produced between 1920 and 1940.

The vast majority of all glassware found was domestic ware, with 53% being from bottles of varying sizes and types, including wine, milk and mineral drink. The second largest category of sherds were from jars, which comprised 43% of the total.

Many of the sherds bear the manufacturers marks of local suppliers, along with some national brands.

Plate 6.24
A selection of the glassware found during recording of the site.

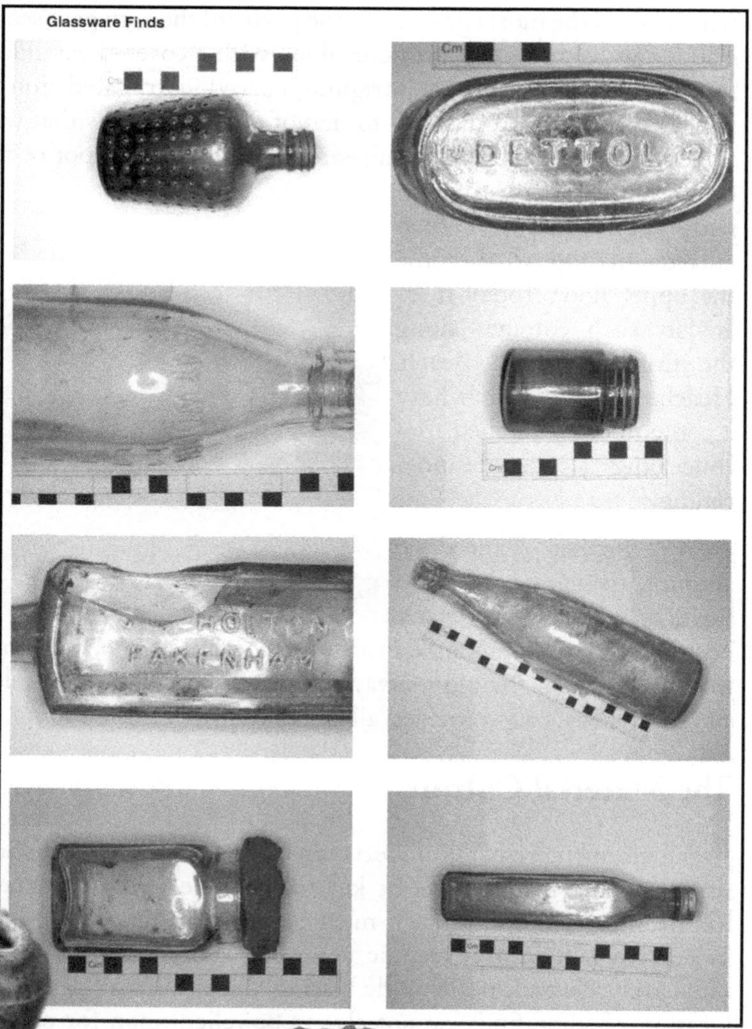

Glassware Finds

Plate 6.25
First World War inkwells found during recording of mortuary building.

Plate 6.26
Undated remains of man's leather boot found during recording area adjacent to mortuary building.

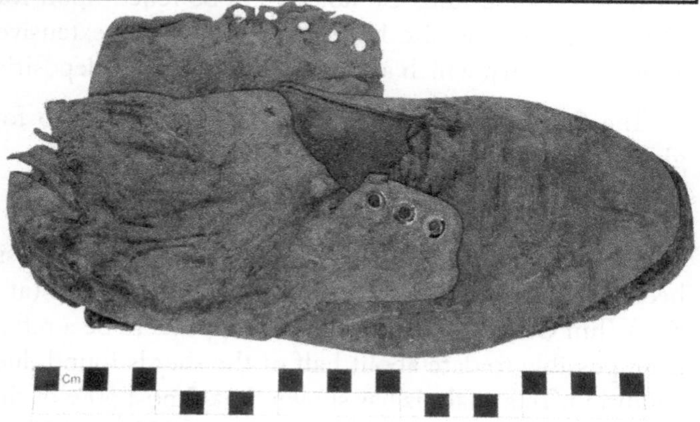

Plate 6.27
One of the many .303 cartridge cases found around the site.

Ceramics

As with glassware, much of the ceramic assemblage appears to relate to domestic use on the site from the pre and post-WWII period. Many of the ceramic sherds were recovered from topsoil adjacent to the WWI squadron office, subsequently used as residential dwellings post- WWII. Several sherds of WWI service ware have been found, along with several complete ink pots, within the western technical area, although these pieces only make up a small proportion of the overall ceramic assemblage.

In all 157 sherds were recovered with ordinary domestic pottery types, such as tablewares and storage jars but also including several sherds of candlestick holders, tending to dominate the assemblage. All of these sherds are of 'modern' (post-1900) date.

Leather

A total of nine leather or textile finds have been recovered from the area to the rear of the WWI squadron office on the southern perimeter of the Whin Close woodland. All were found from within upper contexts, including topsoil, suggesting that the deposit was used for the purpose of rubbish disposal.

Finds of interest include a felt hat, a leather shoe carrying the marking 'Long Buckby Shoes Ltd., 1939', a part of a leather boot which includes metal nails and various lengths of leather straps. These finds suggest domestic occupation of the site shortly after the post-WWII period, when the squadron office was converted into domestic dwellings.

Metal

The metal finds recovered from the site are of three main categories; military (WWI and WWII), domestic (pre and post-WWII) and agricultural (post-WWII). Some finds dating from earlier periods have been recovered during metal detecting survey of the land to the south of the Whin Close woodland which include a Roman Sestertii (Faustina II c.145-175 AD), a post-medieval George II half penny (1727-1760 AD) and a part of a post-medieval buckle (c. 1550-1650 AD).

The finds relating to the site's military use during WWI are predominantly items recovered during recording of the western technical area buildings and as such are of light engineering or mechanical nature, including bolts, nuts, washers, metal plates, copper alloy fragments (some of which show signs of severe heat damage) and tools and engineering instruments. Metal finds of specific interest from this period include: a partial metal identification plate for an Avro 504K aircraft (the plate did not include the aircraft serial number), two Ham & Baker fire hydrant covers, part of a shoulder title badge with letters '...KSHIRE' (possibly relating to the E. Yorkshire Regiment) and a R.F.C. button with royal crest.

A number of .303 cartridge cases have also been recovered from around the site. Most of these are of partial condition, with the manufacturers markings not discernible. The base of a 37mm parachute flare was also covered at the western end of the landing ground. Numerous copper eyelets of varying dimensions have also been recovered from this area, previously used for the placement of a number of Bessonneau hangars.

Eleven part or complete dry cell batteries have been recovered in an upper deposit of the possible rubbish pit at the rear of the WWI squadron offices. Identification has proved difficult but some appear to be from the early 20th century period. The type and quantity of finds recovered suggest that the operational site was comprehensively cleaned before military activity ceased in 1919.

Few WWII metal finds have been recovered by the project; the base of 27mm shell was found at the western end of the landing ground and part of a turtle stove used in the decoy control bunker has been previously recovered. Some electrical cabling from the control bunker has also been recovered by the project.

Many other metal finds relate to domestic occupation of the site during the post-WWII period when disposal of household refuse was not collected by municipal authorities. A number of agricultural implements, such as broken plough tines, have been recovered from the landing ground area, indicating the areas use throughout much of the last century.

Chapter 7

Sedgeford Airfield During World War II

Writing in his book *The Charm of a Village*, Holcombe Ingleby describes that by 1920 Sedgeford aerodrome 'is now a thing of the past'. He recounts how the buildings on the site were dismantled and pulled down towards the end of 1919, although an auction list for the site dated 27th January, 1921 shows many of the aerodrome's buildings still for sale. Regardless, the aerodrome had become silent and much of its land was being put back to agricultural use. However, less than twenty years later World War Two would see the site become operational again but this time it would have a much more clandestine role.

The dark clouds which had started to form over Europe during the mid 1930s had propelled Britain into a concerted programme of expanding its air defences to counter the rapid growth of the German Luftwaffe although it would only be in the immediate months preceding the outbreak of World War Two that consideration would be given for the airfield at Sedgeford's next role.

Under the control of Colonel John Fisher Turner, a former engineer and retired Air Ministry officer, a plan had quickly been conceived to build a system of daytime (K) and night-time (Q) decoy airfield sites. This concept of operating a nationally co-ordinated network of decoy sites arose from the impending threat of Britain being attacked by significant numbers of enemy aircraft flying in large-scale formations and visually acquiring their targets. In addition to repulsing these raids with aerial defence and ground-based anti-aircraft artillery, it had also been proposed that resources would be invested in trying to draw attacking enemy aircraft away from their intended targets by operating realistic decoy sites.

Plate 7.1
Colonel John Turner, architect of Britain's Second World War airfield and factory deception strategy.

From the outset it was viewed that nighttime Q sites would be more effective in distracting enemy aircraft. It was recommended that a typical

Q site would comprise of a ground lighting system that fully replicated that found on a normal airfield, along with its own underground control bunker and telephone communication. For the daytime K sites, it was agreed that purpose-built dummy aircraft were to be used, along with reproduction buildings and features to mimic an operational airfield. Initially, aircraft manufacturers had been approached to submit bids for a range of daytime decoy aircraft. However, all of these manufacturers were in the business of building operational aircraft, not dummies, and the varied quotations they submitted reflected this; the cheapest quotation for a Whitely mock-up being £377 and the most expensive being £1800. All the manufacturers' quotations exceeded the available budget of the Air Ministry and so another avenue had to be explored.

It was not until five days after Britain had officially entered the war that the decoy plan was ready to be activated. During the first days of the war, airfields operated rudimentary nighttime decoys sites using paraffin flares. Under the command of Turner, the Air Ministry's decoy programme hurriedly fell into action. New tenders for dummy aircraft, including replicas of Hurricanes, Battles, and Whitleys, had been quickly drawn up and issued to a completely new set of firms. Foremost amongst those approached were film studios and production companies, such as Warner Brothers and Gaunt British Studios; organisations ideally suited for producing visually realistic replicas.

East Anglia and Lincolnshire, with their large share of forward bomber airfields, were the first regions to receive day decoy sites. These K sites were under the control of four regions, of which the East Anglian region (K3) was based at Mildenhall. Turner envisioned K sites as being of two types. The first comprised a grass field in which take-offs and landings could take place in any direction, the proposed dimensions for this type of site was a maximum of 800 square yards. The second type was where aircraft movements were along defined paths, here two 700 yd. x 200 yd. strips would be configured at right angles. The standard K site would display around ten aircraft and other features such as bomb and petrol dumps, shelters and in some cases building structures would also be created. The objective was to produce a decoy that at 10,000 feet and from six miles out, could pass as an authentic airfield.

By late 1939, four separate production companies were busily engaged producing five different prototype dummy aircraft designs. The company that appeared to have delivered the highest standard of work at the most competitive price was Sound City Films, based at Shepperton. Headed up by Norman Loudon, Sound City had built a decoy Wellington aircraft at the competitive price of £225, and was also working on a Blenheim. Normally engaged in producing sets for a range of different feature films, the studio's team of designers and technicians were used to working to incredibly tight deadlines, a competency that would serve them well with the onset of war. The first production runs began in November 1939, with Sound City being awarded an order to produce 100 Blenheims and 50 Wellingtons. Another studio, Gaumont British, had been given an order for 60 Battles. Green Brothers, a company based near Eastbourne, which had previously manufactured garden furniture, was to provide a 100 Hurricanes.

The dummy aircraft were manufactured in kit form and Sound City had also been given the role of maintaining these aircraft. As such, they established

Plate 7.2
A dummy Spitfire aircraft on display outside Shepperton film studios.

a network of regional depots where the kits were stored prior to issue to the K sites. Sound City staff at these depots also had responsibility for training the site crews in kit assembly. One such depot was based at Beccles in Suffolk. A local resident, Mr Les Baldry, recalls the arrival of Sound City to the locality:

'Our family occupied a house situated in a large yard surrounded by empty malthouse buildings. The property was owned by John Crisp & Sons, maltsters. They employed my father as a foreman maltsterer, although malting in these buildings had just ceased and production had been transferred to their other malting around Beccles.

It was early in the war, whilst I was on leave from RAF flying duties, when a small red lorry arrived unannounced one lunch-time. It was stacked with an assortment of strange cables and equipment. The sign-writing on the doors stated Sound City Films. The tall driver emerged from the cab, introduced himself as Bill Harding and said he had arrived from the London area. He did not reveal the purpose of his arrival and all the equipment was unloaded into the cavernous interior of the empty malthouse. Later on, other mysterious loads arrived. Mr Harding set up offices in the adjoining stables where a telephone was installed.

We never learned what kind of business was being operated from this site by Sound City Films, although we noticed no film stars seemed to come and go. At the end of the hostilities the stores and equipment were removed. I was presented with what I believe to have been an angle of approach projector, that showed yellow, green and red lights, by Bill Harding. In turn I gave him a zipped parachute bag to keep his office papers in when travelling.'

The pressures brought about by the conflict were already seeing any available land turned over to arable use, meaning that decoy sites were often having to be placed on marginal terrain. Ditches often had to be backfilled, although hedgerows were frequently left in place. Many operational airfields painted imitation hedgerows to aid their own camouflage.

Night-time Q sites were much easier to place. Although each Q site's technical and operational plans were defined by Turner's department at the Air Ministry, it was the responsibility of the parent airfield's station commander for choosing site locations. The basis for locating was a requirement that the decoy site had to be approximately 5 miles away from the parent airfield and also aligned along the anticipated enemy flight line. A Q site's operational function was to use a system of electrical lamps mounted on poles, which were laid out in four T-shaped alignments and placed in a cross formation to represent wind indicator lighting. The operational crew would take wind direction readings and set the indicator lights accordingly. Usually added to this were four red obstruction lamps, normally used to identify the proximity of tall buildings and structures, along with a series of glim lights which were used to simulate the angle of glide lighting.

Fig. 7.1
Plan of lighting layout for the Q (nighttime) decoy site at Sedgeford.

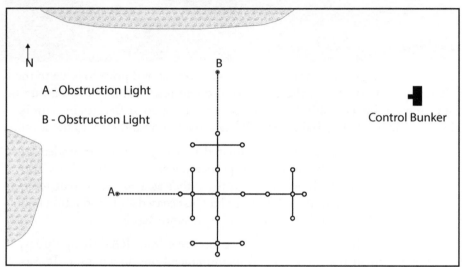

An effective nighttime decoy site may also run the risk of misleading friendly aircraft, so each Q site would use a single recognition light which would be lit in the event that a friendly aircraft mistook it and tried to land. Finally a moveable headlamp, often a car headlight, was affixed to a mount and used to mimic taxiing aircraft. A red Aldis lamp was often used as well. All lights were operated by a central underground control bunker. To be successful in its task, the decoy would try and draw raiding enemy aircraft away from the parent airfield, in the case of Sedgeford (site no. 24b) this being Bircham Newton. Three other Q sites for Bircham Newton were also established at Coxford Heath (site no. 24a), Salthouse (site no. 24c) and Burnham Sutton (site no. 24d).

Plate 7.3
Example of red Aldis signalling lamp on Q sites.

At most K sites, considerable work was required to transform the landscape into a realistic operational site; this also had to include where the crews running the decoy would be accommodated. However, the selection of Sedgeford as a K and Q site enabled this implementation workload to be substantially reduced. The site had previously been a considerable sized aerodrome during WWI, in the later stages it was being developed into a three squadron station. Although many of the original buildings and features had been removed after the Armistice, some buildings still remained in place at the outbreak of WWII. Just as importantly, the cropmarks formed by many of the earlier site's original features were remarkably clear, giving a credible picture of an operational airfield, or of one in the process of development.

It is believed that the K site was the first element to become operational at

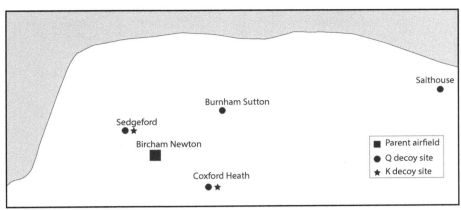

Fig. 7.2
Map of decoy sites for parent site RAF Bircham Newton airfield.

Sedgeford, although an exact date is not known. We know that by June 1940, 51 Q sites had become operational throughout the rest of the country. While a general uniform template was used for the construction of Q site control bunkers, there appear many variations both regionally and nationally in the design and materials actually used. There appears to be a pattern of earlier control bunkers being built using the 'cut and cover' method; a large trench being excavated and the bunker built using cast concrete and metal corrugated sheeting before being backfilled with earth. Later control bunkers appear to be constructed at ground level using brick or precast concrete and then covered with earth banking. The Q site at Sedgeford is of the earlier design.

Although an exact date for the establishment of the Sedgeford decoy site is not known, the neighbouring decoy site at Coxford Heath, also part of the Bircham Newton decoy network, was selected on 19th September, 1939. Groundwork would have been undertaken by personnel from Bircham Newton, with site lighting and equipment installed by the Air Ministry Directorate of Works.

At operational airfields, such as Bircham Newton, significant work was also undertaken to conceal its function. Hangars were camouflaged to blend in with the landscape and a series of hedgerows were painted onto the airfield itself. Some of these measures were to prove more effective than others but the dummy hedgerows appeared to be incredibly realistic and would easily have passed for the real thing as seen from an aircraft flying at operational height and speed.

It is not known exactly which buildings and features from the WWI aerodrome were still in place at Sedgeford at the outbreak of WWII and which may have been used to form part of the decoy airfield. An aerial photograph of the site, taken during the early part of 1946, does show two of the G.S. sheds still in situ. One of these is Shed No 2, on the eastern side of the site, the other being Shed No. 3, on the south-west edge of the airfield. Another undated aerial photograph, taken later during 1946, shows both of these hangars having been dismantled. The photographs also show the WWI squadron offices and technical store, along with numerous smaller, unidentified buildings. The original roadways and a number of other trackways can be clearly be seen. Married with some additional fabricated buildings and features and with dummy aircraft on display (at Sedgeford three dummy Hudson aircraft were used), viewed from the skies, Sedgeford would have had the appearance of an operational airfield.

Fig. 7.3
Site plan of Q/K decoy site at
Sedgeford during WWII.

1. WWI G.S. shed (No.3)
2. Landing light area for decoy airfield
3. Decoy (K) site accommodation building
   (WWI squaron office)
4. Latrines
5. Unknown building
6. Unknown building
7. Decoy (K) site shelter
8. WWI mortuary building
9. WWI technical store
10. Unknown building

11. Unknown building
12. Unknown building
13. WWI motor transport shed
14. WWI workshop building
15. WWI G.S. shed (No.2)
16. WWI G.S. shed (No.1)
17. Home Guard firing range
18. Area containing anti-glider
    landing trenches
19. Caravan for Q site
20. Q site control bunker

Some of the buildings from the site's WWII role still remain in place today. Approximately 10 metres to the rear of the WWI squadron office building is an underground shelter. The structure consists of a brick walled rectangle, with a concrete slab roof and a concrete floor. The whole building is recessed into the surrounding ground, with approximately half of the building's height being above original ground level. The roof consists of single cast concrete of 6 inch thickness, cast in-situ and utilising a base of galvanised cast iron sheeting. The top slab had a rebated edge, raised 2 inches to retain a clay/topsoil covering.

Plate 7.4
The exterior of the shelter
adjacent to accommodation
building at the Sedgeford
K site. The building in
the upper right of the
photograph is the WWI
mortuary

Plate 7.5
Interior of shelter building
for Sedgeford K site.

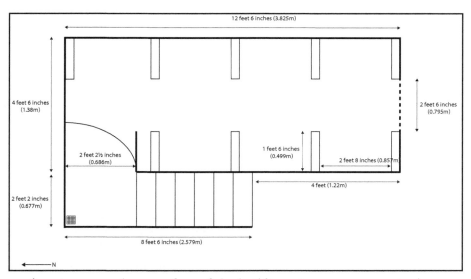

Fig. 7.4
Plan of shelter building for
Sedgeford K site

A staircase on the west face of the building gives access to a single room measuring 12 feet, 6 inches by four feet six inches, set upon a concrete slab of approximately 3 inch thickness. The shelter had a drain built into the north west corner of the base of the stairwell. Within this room were 8 brick piers to support wooden benches, where it was estimated that 12 to 16 persons could be seated. There exists a roughly hewn 'window' in the south elevation of the shelter, suggesting that this may not be part of the original feature. The opening features a concrete lintel but shows evidence of being refilled and then subsequently re-opened. The possibility arises that the shelter could have been reutilised post-WWII when the nearby squadron offices were converted to domestic dwellings. The brickwork of the shelter is contemporary to that of the underground control bunker on the eastern side of the site, suggesting that this feature was added at the beginning of WWII and would have been used by members of the site crew when using the officers' quarters building.

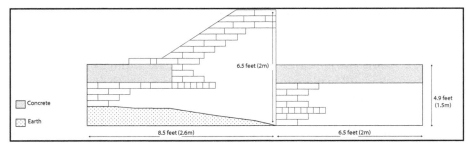

Fig. 7.5
Drawing of west facing
elevation of shelter building
at Sedgeford K site.

On the eastern side of the Whin Close woodland, close to the landing target marker of the WWI airfield, is a small patch of set-aside grassland within the contemporary arable crop. This would have been the centre for Sedgeford's nocturnal operational role during WWII; the location of the Q site control bunker.

Viewing the area today, only a small section of a ceramic duct, which protrudes through the undergrowth, can be seen from any distance. Only when you are almost standing on top of it does the outline of the bunker appear. It is believed that the ceramic duct may have been used as a flue for a 'Tortoiseshell' stove, which would have been used for heating food and keeping warm. A large fragment from the actual stove used at Sedgeford can be found

Fig. 7.6
Plan of Sedgeford Q site
control bunker.

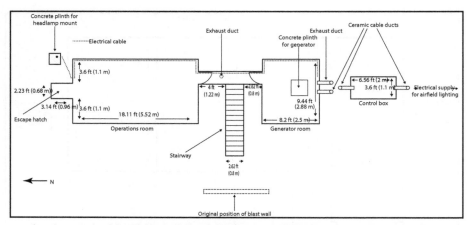

on display at the Norfolk and Suffolk Aviation Museum near Bungay, Suffolk. The placement of the duct, located in a small passageway at the bottom of the staircase and outside both control and generator rooms, still raises questions as to its function.

Plate 7.6
Entrance stairway to the Q
site control bunker.

Plate 7.7
Large fragment of the
original 'Tortoiseshell' stove
which was used in the control
bunker at the Q site at
Sedgeford.

Entry to the bunker is made by a central concrete staircase which descends underground, with two rooms (control and generator) leading off either side at the bottom of the stairs. Only door frames remain for both control and generator rooms and appear to have been built to take ordinary wooden doors (one of which is still in place in the aforementioned K site shelter). Plans for Q control bunkers of this period show a single course brick blast wall directly in front of the stair entrance. No evidence remains of one at this bunker, although it is highly likely that this has been previously removed. Around the roof of the stairway access, the mortar remains of a single brick course can be seen which may have originally been part of a protective cover.

The substantial shelter structure was of 'cut and cover' construction; excavating a deep trench and then pouring concrete into the excavated area for floors and walls. Cast corrugated iron casings were then affixed to the concrete base to form ceilings for both rooms. The iron casing still bears the manufacturer's nameplate of Joseph Westwood & Co., Napier Yard, Millwall, London E4. With the corrugated casings in place, a four feet, nine inches thick layer of concrete was then poured on top of the casing. Once set, this was then backfilled with a further three foot layer of topsoil.

The control bunker is aligned north-south. To the south is the generator room, measuring nine feet, five inches in length by eight feet, two inches wide and six feet, nine inches in height. Situated in the centre of the generator room is a square concrete plinth with four iron affixing bolts embedded into the concrete. The plinth would have been used to house the generator (an Austin 8 HP engine was frequently used for this purpose) which produced the site's power. Two large ceramic ducts are set into the southern wall of the generator room. The ducts reappear slightly below ground level on the surface; one being used to feed out the generator exhaust pipe, the other contained the electrical output cable which would have fed the site's lighting arrays. Hidden by thick undergrowth around these ducts, lies a concrete base with a surrounding single course of bricks, measuring six feet, six inches by three feet, three inches. This feature would have been used as a junction box, taking the output cable from the generator and then converting to electrical cabling for the rest of the site. The diesel generator would have produced enough power to feed wind T lights, obstruction lights and the moveable headlamp.

Plate 7.8
The electrical junction box located above the control bunker. The ceramic exhaust duct can be seen above the junction box.

Plate 7.9
Interior the bunker's control room. A stairwell can be seen the at northern end of room which would have been used to operate the moveable headlamp which was mounted to a concrete base above the bunker.

The room situated to the north is the control room, measuring 18 feet, 11 inches in length by nine feet, four inches wide and six feet, eight inches high. A vertical stairwell leading to the surface is built into its northernmost wall. The metal footrungs have been removed from the stairwell but it is still sealed by its original iron hatch. About one metre to the east of the hatch is the partial remains of a concrete base, measuring two feet by two feet. The truncated metal frame of the metal headlamp mounting frame still protrudes from the base; from which a length of electrical cable still runs through the frame into the earth and then through a conduit into the control room. Cable mountings ran along the eastern wall of the control room, taking the cable to the adjoining generator.

Within the control room a two man team, in telephone communication with the station commander at Bircham Newton and operating on alternate watches, would have manned the site. When an alert was received, the generator was started, field lights switched on and one of the team would then use the headlamp to mimic a taxiing aircraft until the enemy was close enough to pick up the landing T's on the ground. One of the team would also hold a red Aldis signalling lamp to replicate warnings to approaching aircraft.

While K and Q sites performed the role of decoys to attacking enemy aircraft, the manner in which sites carried out this task was essentially different. Once set up, the K site had a more passive role, with aircraft regularly moved to show signs of activity. However, the role of a Q site was much more dynamic

with the focus being to try and actively draw nighttime bombers to the site. In a communiqué to station commanders, Colonel Turner had outlined operational procedures in the event of an air raid warning being issued:

'The operation staff at the parent station will ring up the night dummy. Here there will be two men provided each night by the parent station taking watch. One will probably be asleep. The man on watch wakes his companion and starts up the generator. When the generator has been started up, one man goes to the control panel and switches on the correct T, the obstruction lights and the head lamp. The two men take it in turns to manipulate the headlamp until an aircraft is heard approaching near enough to pick up the landing T. They will then switch it out and stand on watch. If the aircraft is a friend and signals by a Very light he wants to land, i.e. he mistakes the Q lighting for a real aerodrome, the lights are switched off. If it is an enemy who starts to attack, the obstruction lights only are switched off and the T flare is left because on stations and satellites T flare paths cannot be extinguished in a sudden attack without great risk to personnel. The two men then take cover in their dugout and report.'

Additional instructions were given in operating the headlamp to accurately mimic a taxiing aircraft. The lamp was to be first rotated through 90 degrees, taking five seconds. The lamp was then to be switched off for 40 seconds, moved in a different direction and a further sweep completed.

One of the operating crew at Sedgeford, Mr Len Douglass, remembers his time at the decoy site during WWII.

'Sedgeford was one of the decoy airfield sites for RAF Bircham Newton, where I served pre-war. Sedgeford was a World War One aerodrome with one of its hangars surviving, together with smaller buildings. The hangar was used by the decoy crew for erecting the dummy aircraft in before dispersing them around the site. Next to the underground bunker, on the east side of the site, was a wooden caravan with four solid wheels that was used by the crew. One of my roles when on night duty, was to flash a red Aldis lamp at German aircraft: a flashing red light meant "do not land - another aircraft in circuit" and was used to attract bombers to our decoy. I later served on the Coxford decoy site.'

Roland Axman, a resident who lived in Sedgeford throughout the war, also has memories of the site:

'As young lads, we used to go as near as we could to see what was going on. There were a few dummy aeroplanes about but it was that red beacon that flashed every night and the odd Lysander that landed there that was of interest to us. Large fields nearby were trenched to deter planes from landing.'

There appears to be little evidence for the decoy site at Sedgeford suffering direct attack apart from once being strafed by enemy aircraft. Certainly the local area saw significant enemy bombing, with the Rural District of Docking, which encompassed an area of north west Norfolk as far south as West Rudham, suffering 65 days of bombing during WWII with just over 72 tonnes of bombs being dropped on the area. The focus of these attacks would have been the airfields at Bircham Newton and Docking. In comparison to Sedgeford, the Q/K site at Coxford Heath, located between Syderstone and Tattersett, attracted considerably more enemy attention. Dummy hangars, buildings and bomb dumps, along with dummy Hudson aircraft, were placed to the south of Coxford Wood. The decoy site at Coxford Heath was operated by a crew of eleven men, with an NCO in charge, who made use of a nearby gamekeeper's cottage as their billet. Records for Coxford Heath show that it was bombed on 60 occasions during 1940, as opposed to 28 on Bircham Newton itself.

In addition to the decoy sites attached to RAF Bircham Newton, 24 other such decoy sites were located throughout Norfolk. Many of the control bunkers for these sites have been lost over the years, yet others still remain, some being in relatively good order. At Wormegay (site 27c), which served both Marham and Downham Market airfields, the control bunker (an above the ground design) is still in relatively good order.

Plate 7.12 (left) Q site control bunker at Wormegay, Norfolk (27C). This bunker is of different design and construction materials to that used at Sedgeford.

Plate 7.13 (right) Q site control bunker at Great Gidding, Cambridgeshire (130A) showing the variation in designs and materials used for construction of decoy sites.

Anecdotal accounts describe an additional feature to the site's WWII role in the shape of a series of anti-glider trenches that were created in the field opposite of Pump Cottages along the B1454 Sedgeford to Docking Road. The field, measuring almost a 1,000 metres in length and 350 metres wide, adjoins the northern area of the WWI aerodrome site. The size and relative flatness of the field making it an ideal landing site. The accounts investigated, describe a series of five to six trenches being dug in the field on the opposite side of the

Plate 7.14
Entrance stairway to
Q site control bunker
at Warmington,
Northamptonshire (97A).

Plate 7.15
Interior of control
room at Warmington,
Northamptonshire Q site.

Plate 7.16
Entrance stairway to Q site
control bunker at Maxey,
Cambridgeshire (34A).

Plate 7.14
Entrance stairway to
Q site control bunker
at Warmington,
Northamptonshire (97A).

Plate 7.15
Interior of control
room at Warmington,
Northamptonshire Q site.

Plate 7.16
Entrance stairway to Q site
control bunker at Maxey,
Cambridgeshire (34A).

road from Pump Cottages. This would place the trenches towards the western field boundary, so there is the likelihood that further trenches may have been placed eastwards across the field. The trenches were backfilled before the end of the war and do not appear on 1946 aerial photographs of the area. At the time of writing, the site has not been surveyed to locate these features.

Another function of the Sedgeford site's WWII role has proved harder to establish. Several local residents have referred to a field to the south east of the airfield, lower down the valley towards Fring, as being known as 'Searchlight Field'. A hand-drawn 'memory' map, produced by a local resident whose father worked at the aerodrome during WWI, does include a searchlight battery. However, no records from the WWI period refer to the aerodrome as having searchlights present on site. There is perhaps some confusion on the part of the author of the map with the aerodrome during WWII, where a searchlight battery may well have been present nearby. 431 Battery at Bircham Newton operated two such troops during the war. Aerial photographs taken during 1946 do indicate a possible feature in the area suggested. The feature appears to be an area of hard standing used to mount the searchlights. Anecdotal accounts describes four to five temporary timber huts, an anti-aircraft gun and searchlight being present on the site. At the time of writing, this feature remains under investigation.

One final feature from the original Sedgeford aerodrome which was used throughout WWII was the machine gun target range. Originally built to train airmen how to operate the Lewis gun on their aircraft, the range was utilised throughout WWII by the local Home Guard unit for rifle target practice.

Appendix 1 – H.S. Wolff Flight Log

Date	Pilot	Machine Type & No.	Passenger	Time	Height	Course	Remarks
3/6/17	Self	H.F.	Lt. Duffers	20	500	Sedgeford	1st dual in Henri Farman.
4/6/17	Lt. Duffers	FE2b	Self	30	4,000	"	Reconnaisance.
6/6/17	"	FE2b	Self	30	4,000	"	Cross country.
25/6/17	Lt. Meek	Avro	Self	15	3,000	"	1st joy ride in Avro.
26/6/17	Lt. Beinge	Avro	Self	15	6,000	"	Dual control.
28/6/17	Cpt. Sandys	Avro	Self	25	4,000	"	Dual control.
6/7/17	Cpt. Bell	Avro	Self	20	2,000	"	Dual could not turn
12/7/17	Lt. Angus	Avro	Self	35	4,000	"	Dual control..
17/7/17	Lt. Meek	Avro	Self	20	2,000	"	Took off and landed.
24/7/17	Cpt. McClintock	Avro	Self	25	300	"	Dual landings.
24/7/17	Cpt. McClintock	Avro	Self	15	200	"	Dual landings.
24/7/17	Self	Avro	–	10	2.000	"	1st solo in Avro.
25/7/17	Self	Avro	–	46	5.000	"	Stalled and spiralled.
25/5/17	Self	Avro	–	20	5,000	"	"
25/7/17	Self	Avro	–	40	4,000	"	Side slipped.
26/7/17	Self	Avro	–	25	3,500	"	Very bumpy.
26/7/17	Self	Avro	–	30	3,000	"	Misty. Tried to spin.
27/7/17	Lt. Lutyens	Avro	Self	40	3,000	"	Immeirmans and spins
28/7/17	Self	Avro	–	20	2,500	"	"
16/8/17	Lt. Angus	Avro	Self	30	3,000	"	My first experience of loop.

Appendix 2 – Airfields in Norfolk During the First World War

RNAS

Burgh Castle, 1915-19, NLG
Bacton, 1915-18, NLG
Great Yarmouth, South Denes, 1911-18, SAS
Hickling Broad, 1916-18, SLG
Holt , 1916-18, NLG
Pulham, 1915-18, AS
Sedgeford, 1915-17, NLG

RFC/RAF

Bircham Newton, 1918-62, TDS, BB
Earsham, 1916-19, HD, LG
Feltwell, 1917-20, TDS
Freethorpe, 1916-18, LG
Gooderstone, 1916-18, LG, HD
Harling Road, 1916-20, HD, NLG, TDS
Hingham, 1916-19, HD
Horstead with Stanninghall, 1916-18, LG
Marham, 1916-19 , LG, HD, TA
Marsham, 1915-16, LG
Mattishall, 1915-19, HD
Mousehold Heath, 1915-19, HD, LG, AAP (Aircraft Acceptance
    Park), ARS, TDS
Narborough, 1915-19, TA, TDS
North Elmham, 1916-?, LG
Saxthorpe, 1916-18, LG
Scoulton, 1917, HD
Tibenham, 1916-19, LG
Snarehill, 1916-19, HD, TDS, RAFS, ARS
Sporle, 1916-18, LG
Sedgeford, 1915-20, TA, TDS
West Rudham, 1916-18, LG

NLG - Night Landing Ground
AS - Airship Station
SAS - Seaplane and Aeroplane Station
SLG - Seaplane Landing Ground
TA - Training Airfield
TDS - Training Depot Station
BS - Bomber Station
HD - Home Defence
RAFS - RAF School
ARS - Aeroplane Repair Section
AAP - Aircraft Acceptance Park

Appendix 3 – Norfolk WWII Decoy Sites

Decoy Site	No.	Type	Parent
Terrington St. Clements	23a	Q	Sutton Bridge
Coxford Heath	24a	Q/K	Bircham Newton
Sedgeford	24b	Q/K	Bircham Newton
Salthouse	24c	Q	Bircham Newton
Burnham Sutton	24d	Q	Bircham Newton
Fulmodeston	25a	Q/K	West Raynham
Gately	25b	Q	West Raynham
North Tuddenham	26a	Q/K	Swanton Morley
Swaffham	27a	Q/K	Marham
South Acre	27b	Q	Marham
Wormegay	27c	Q	Marham
Thetford	28a	Q/K	Honington
Lakenheath	29a	Q/K	Feltwell
Stanford	29b	Q	Feltwell
Southery	29c	Q	Feltwell
Cavenham	30a	Q/K	Mildenhall
Littleport	30b	Q	Mildenhall
Beeston St. Lawrence	53a	Q	Coltishall
Suffield	53b	Q	Coltishall
Crostwick	54a	Q	Horsham St. Faith
Fulmodeston	114a	Q	Foulsham
Warham St. Mary	119b	Q	Langham
Salthouse	119a	Q	Langham
North Creake	149a	Q	Docking
Burnham Sutton	149b	Q	Docking
Brandon	165a	Q	Lakenheath
West Bradenham	169a	Q	Watton
Breckles	169b	Q	Watton
Hempnall	172a	Q	Hardwick
Coxford Heath	186a	Q	Sculthorpe
South Acre	191a	Q	Downham Market
Wormegay	191b	Q	Downham Market
Little Plumstead	C33a	QL	Norwich
Little Plumstead	SF43a	SF	Norwich
Bramerton	C33b	QL	Norwich
Bramerton	SF43b	SF	Norwich
Horning	C33c	QL	Norwich
Horning	SF43c	SF	Norwich
Winterton Ness	YA1	NSF/NQL	Great Yarmouth
Lound	YA2	NSF/NQL	Great Yarmouth
Burgh St. Peter	N10/LO1	NSF/NQL	Lowestoft

Possible Decoy Sites (official references and authentication of site not obtained at publication date)
Docking
Barton Bendish
Gooderstone Warren
Hillborough
Poringland
Shotesham

Q - Night decoy site for airfield
K - Day decoy site for airfield
SF - Civil Starfish decoy site
QL - Civil lighting decoy site
NQL - Naval lighting decoy site
NSF– Naval Starfish decoy site

Appendix 4 – World War One Wireless Stations

Alnwick, Northumberland (Admiralty)
Beaumanor Hall, Leicestershire (Admiralty)
Berwick, Northumberland (Admiralty)
Birchington/St. Nicholas at Wade, Kent (Admiralty)
Bolt Head, Devon (GPO
Broomfield, Essex (Admiralty)
Caister-on-Sea, Norfolk (GPO)
Cambridge, Cambridgeshire
Cawood, North Yorkshire (Admiralty)
Chelmsford, (Essex) (Marconi/Lloyds)
Cirencester, Gloucestershire
Cleethorpes, Lincolnshire (Admiralty)
Crosby Battery, Merseyside (Admiralty)
Cullercoats, North Tyneside (Admiralty)
Culver Cliff, Isle of Wight (Admiralty)
Devizes, Wiltshire (Admiralty)
Doncaster, South Yorkshire
Dover Castle, Kent (Admiralty)
Dover - Citadel, Kent (Garrison/Army)
Dover - Langdon, Kent (Garrison/Army)
Farnborough, Hampshire
Felixstowe, Suffolk (Admiralty)
Feltham, Middlesex
Flamborough Head, East Riding of Yorkshire (Admiralty)
Folkestone, Kent
Fort Blockhouse, Gosport, Hampshire (Admiralty)
Frenchman's Point, Tyneside (Garrison/Army)
Heysham Harbour, Lancashire (Railway Company)
Horsea Island, Portsmouth (Admiralty)
Hounslow, Middlesex
Hunstanton, Norfolk (Admiralty)
Isle Of Grain, Kent (Garrison/Army)
Land's End, Cornwall (Admiralty)
Leafield, Oxfordshire (Marconi/Lloyds)
Lizard, Cornwall (Admiralty/Lloyds)
London, The Strand (Admiralty)
London, Whitehall (Admiralty)
Lowestoft, Suffolk (Admiralty)
Lydd, Kent (Admiralty)
Maidstone, Kent
Malvern, Worcestershire (Admiralty)
Mersey Dock And Harbour Board Vessels X 5 (Admiralty)

Narborough, Leicestershire
Neston, Cheshire
Newcastle-Upon-Tyne, Tyne And Wear
Newhaven, East Sussex (Railway Company)
Niton, Isle Of Wight (Marconi/Lloyds)
Nodes Point, Isle Of Wight (Garrison/Army)
North Foreland, Kent
Norton, Worcestershire
Norwich, Norfolk
Parkestone Quay, Essex (Railway Company)
Perch Rock Battery, Merseyside (Garrison/Army)
Peterborough, Cambridgeshire
Pevensey, East Sussex (Admiralty)
Poldhu, Cornwall (Marconi/Lloyds)
Poole, Dorset (Marconi/Lloyds)
Portland Bill, Dorset (Admiralty)
Portsmouth Signal School, Hampshire
Prawle Point, Devon (Admiralty)
Puckpool, Isle Of Wight (Garrison/Army)
Rame Head, Cornwall (Admiralty)
Ravelin Battery, Kent (Garrison/Army)
Sandwich, Kent (Admiralty)
Scarborough, North Yorkshire (Admiralty)
Seaforth, Merseyside (GPO)
Seaham, County Durham
Sedgeford (aerodrome), Norfolk
Sheerness, Kent (Admiralty)
Slough Fort, Isle Of Grain, Kent (Garrison/Army)
South Carlton, Lincolnshire
Southsea Castle, Hampshire (Garrison/Army)
Spurn Head, East Riding of Yorkshire (Garrison/Army)
Stockton-on-Tees, County Durham (Admiralty)
Trevose, Cornwall
Tynemouth Castle, Tyne and Wear (Garrison/Army)
Warden Point Battery, Isle of Wight (Garrison/Army)
Withern Sea, East Riding of Yorkshire
Woolwich Common, Greater London
Worcester, Worcestershire
Worthy Down, Hampshire (Garrison/Army)
York, North Yorkshire (Admiralty)

Appendix 5 – Representative Aircraft (inc. a/c reference numbers) of Squadrons based at Sedgeford Aerodrome

45 Squadron RFC/RAF

Representative Aeroplanes (* joined BEF with the unit)

Avro 504	793, 2890, 4027, 4047, 4048, 4052, 4065, 4066, 4069, 4759.
Bristol Scout C	5294.
Bristol Scout D	5560, 5567.
HF F.20	568, 2845, 2484, 7408, 7412.
Martinsyde S1	5442, 5452.
RAF BE2b	2179.
RAF BE2c	1659, 1761, 2062, 2069, 2073, 2079, 2081, 2478, 2712, 4473, 4474, 4744, 5402, 5403.
RAF BE12	6481.
RAF FE2b	4957.
Sopwith 1½ Strutter	A7774*, 7775*, 7776*, 7777*, 7778*, 7779*, 7780*, 7782*, 7783*, 7786*, 7788*, A1061, A1064*, A1066*, A1069*, A1070*.
Vickers FB5	5660, 7515.

64 Squadron RFC/RAF

Representative Aeroplanes (* to BEF with the unit)

AMC DH1A	4620.
AMC DH5	A9237*, A9316*, A9393, A9481*, A9490*, A9486*, A9507*.
Avro 504A	A5923, A8587, B929, B936, B956, B957, B994, B3183, B3212, B3216.
HF F.20	7412, 7434, 7435, 7436, 7437, A1177, A1179, A1189, A1202, A1229, A1233, A1722, A1731, A1732.
RAF FE2b	4276, 4279, 4888, 4893, 4950, 6957, 6958, 6960, 6961, 6962.
Sopwith Pup	A7311, B1778, B1786, B1787, B1788, B1789, B1839, B9440.

53 Reserve/Training Squadron RFC/RAF

Representative Aeroplanes

AMC DH6	A9607, A9608, A9610, A9669, A9733, A9754, B2634, B2667, B2668, B2669, B2763, C2020, C6806.
Avro 504B	A9975.
Avro 504A/J	A8520, B957, D8832.
RAF BE2e	A1275, A1276, A1812, A1813, A1814, A1816, A1851, A2794, A2793, A2794, A2832, A2969, A2974, A3057, A3115, B4442, B4571, B9998.
RAF RE8	A3189, A3641, A3879, A3881, A4546, B6669, D4724.

65 Reserve/Training Squadron RFC/RAF

Representative Aeroplanes

Avro 504A/J	7991, A8583, A8585, A8587, B756, B929, B956, B957, B992, B993, B994, B4340, B4362, B8708, B8987, D49, D53, D113, D114, D132.
AW FK3	A1494.
AW FK8	B297.
Bristol Scout D	A1779.
Martinsyde G.102	A3995.
RAF BE2e	6734, 7214, A1864, A1868, A2930, A2969, A2980, A8641, B790, B4006, B4009, B4524.
RAF RE8	A3419, A3479, A3486, A4587, A4684.
Sopwith Pup	B5312, B5297, B6069, B8786, C3502, D4080.
Sopwith F1 Camel	B6315, B6395, B8830, B9146.

87 Squadron RFC/RAF

Representative Aeroplanes (* to BEF with the unit)

Avro 504A/J	A3395, A8509, B3183, B4218, B4252, B4255.
RAF SE5a	B648, B4892, C9547, C9558.
Sopwith Pup	B1758, B1789, B1804, B1812, B2187, B2230, B2248, B2250, B5251, B5252, B5256, B5313, B5324, B5353, B5360, B5376, B5384, B5389, B5903, B7381, B9440, B9931, C273, C8653.
Sopwith F1 Camel	
Sopwith Dolphin	C3912*, C4056*, C4155*, C4156*, C4157*, C4158*, C4159*, C4161*, C4162*, C4163*, C4165*, C4166*, C4167*, C4168*, C4173*, C4174*, C4176*, C4177*, C4178*, C8163*.

72 Squadron RFC

Representative Aeroplanes

Avro 504A	A476, A1972, A5912, A5915, A9784.
Sopwith Pup	B5901, B5903.
SPAD S.VII	A8832.

110 Squadron RFC/RAF

Representative Aeroplanes (* to IF with the unit)

AMC DH4	A7734, A7793, A7965, B9994.
AMC DH6	A9611, A9616, B9031, C2139, C6504.
AMC DH9	B6063, B6076, B6088, B6089, C1011, C1162, C6071, C6073, C6076, C6089, C6126, D2779, D3117, D5686, D5686, D5689, E603.
AMC DH9A	E8410*, E9660*, E9661, F977*, F978*, F980*, F981*, F983, F984, F985*, F986*, F988, F989, F991, F992*, F993*, F995*, F996*, F997*, F1000*, F1004*, F1005*, F1010*.
AW FK3	B9565, B9584, B9585, B9596, B9616, B9617, 9619, B9625, B9627.
AW FK8	C8611, C8636.
Martinsyde G.102	A3996, A3997, A6255, A6269, A6272, A6280, 6296, A6298, A6299, B860, B864, B865, B866, B872, B873, B874.
RAF BE2d	5747.
RAF BE2e	7207, A2980, B4006, B4009, B4524. B4547, B4550, B4559, B4561, B4570.
RAF RE8	B824.

122 Squadron RFC/RAF

Representative Aeroplanes

AMC DH6	A9737, A9739, A9740, A9741, B2669, C6581, C6598, C6607, C6802.
AMC DH9	B6071, B6096, B6098, D1651, D1698, D1705.
AW FK3	B9583, B9584, B9611, B9627, B9643.
Martinsyde G.102	A6299, B860, B872, B874.
RAF RE8	A3471, A3735, A3888, B829, D4997

9 Training Squadron RFC/RAF

Representative Aeroplanes

AMC DH1A	4604, 4619.
AMC DH4	A7491, A7496, A7504, A7506, A7604, A7649, A7662, A7667, A7717, A7752, A7793, B2054, B5452, B9951.
AMC DH9	B9359, B9360, D5556.
Avro 504D	799.
AW FK3	A1503, A8126, B9562, B9563, B9564.

Caudron G.III	5035, 5043, 5052, 5053.
HF F.20	565, 7398, 7399, A1199, A1214.
Martinsyde S.1	2449, 2831, 4249.
MF Se.7	418, 535, 2957, 2976, 2980, 2982, 2999, 4012, 4014, 4015, 5617, 6697, 6698
MF Se.11	A2468, A4257, 7364, 7365.
RAF BE2c	1720, 2670, 2718.
RAF BE2d	5747.
RAF BE2e	7188, 8723, A3111, A8723, B4403, B4404.
RAF FE2b	4264, 4277, 4910, 4923, 4953, 5229, 6956, 6959, 7667, 7668, 7688, A6361.
RAF RE8	A3891, A3897, A3898, A3921, B5132.
Vickers FB5	1622, 1628, 2342, 5665.

3 Fighting School RAF

Representative Aeroplanes

AMC DH4	B2100.
AMC DH9	D7332, D7372.
AMC DH9A	E9667.
Avro 504J/K	B3202, C746, C749, C750, D6201, D6202, D6203, D6204, D6205, D6207, E3427, E3444, E3445, E3448, E3449, E3450, E3472, E3473, E3487.
Bristol F2B	C9866, C9867, D8067, D8073, D8074.
Bristol M1C	C5022, C5023, C5024, C5025.
HP 0/400	F248.
RAF BE2e	6786.
RAF SE5a	F7964, F7969.
Sopwith Triplane	N5910.
Sopwith Pup	C417.
Sopwith F1 Camel	B5582, B9292, C91, C168, C169, C185, C186, C187, C8317, C8318, C8320, D8226, E1474, E7236, E7237, E7239, E7251, E7253, E7254, E7257, F3096, 2200, H2724.

Appendix 6 – Sedgeford Squadrons Timeline

R.N.A.S.

> Night Landing Ground for Great Yarmouth, South Denes
> Arrival date - August, 1915
> Departure date - May, 1916

45 Squadron

> Arrival date - 21st May, 1916
> From - Thetford
> Departure date - 12th October, 1916
> To - St. Omer, France

64 Squadron

> Formed at Sedgeford
> Arrival date - 1st August, 1916
> Departure date - 14th October, 1917
> To - France

53 Reserve Squadron

> Formed at Sedgeford
> Arrival date - 1st February, 2017
> Departure date - 14th February, 1917
> To - Narborough

65 Training Squadron

> Arrival date - 10th May, 1917
> From - Croydon
> Departure date - 25th November, 1917
> To - Dover

87 Squadron

> Arrival date - 15th September, 1917
> From - Upavon
> Departure date - 19th December, 1917
> To - Hounslow

72 Squadron

> Arrival date - 1st November, 1917
> From - Netheravon
> Departure date - 25th December, 1917
> To - Mesopotamia

110 Squadron

Arrival date - 26th November, 1917
From - Swingate Down
Departure date - 15th June, 1918
To - Kenley

122 Squadron

Formed at Sedgeford
Arrival date - 1st January, 1918
Disbanded at Sedgeford - 17th August, 1918

9 Training Squadron

Arrival date - 10th January, 1918
From - Mousehold Heath
Departure date - August, 1918
To - Tallaght, Ireland

24 Aero Squadron

Arrival date - 31st January, 1918
From - Romney Rest Camp, Winchester
Departure date - 1st May, 1918
To - Narborough

3 Fighting School

Arrival date - November, 1918
From - Bircham Newton
Re-designated 7 Training School 14th March, 1919

13 Squadron Cadre

Arrival date - 27th March, 1919
From - St. Omer, France
Disbanded 31st December, 1919

60 Squadron

Arrival date - 28th February, 1919
From - Rhineland, Germany
Disbanded 22nd January, 1920

7 Training School

Redesigned from 3 Fighting School 14th March, 1919
Disbanded October, 1919

Appendix 7 – Zeppelin L–3

Builder's No.	LZ 24
Builder's Type	M
Owner	German Navy
Operational Name	L–3
First Flight	11th May, 1914
Vol.	22,497.3 m3
Length	157.937 m
Diameter	14.783 m
Gas cells	18
Unladen weight	16,896 kgs
Payload	9,185 kgs
Engines	3 x Maybach C-X six-cylinder
Total H.P.	630
Speed	76.3 km/h

Appendix 8 – Zeppelin L4

Builder's No.	LZ 27
Builder's Type	M
Owner	German Navy
Operational Name	L4
First Flight	28th August, 1914
Vol.	22,497.3 m3
Length	157.93m
Diameter	14.78m
Gas cells	18
Unladen weight	16,896 kgs
Payload	9,117 kgs
Engines	3 x Maybach C-X six-cylinder
Total H.P.	630
Speed	82.72 km/h

Appendix 9 – Zeppelin L70

Builder's No.	LZ 112
Builder's Type	X
Owner	German Navy
Operational No.	L70
First Flight	1st July, 1918
Vol.	62178.13 m3
Length	211.5m
Diameter	23.93m
Gas cells	15
Payload	44,043.81 kgs
Engines	7 x Maybach IVa
Total H.P.	81
Speed	130.35 km/h

Appendix 10 – Resumé of Work May 1918 – Nov 1918

C O M M U N I Q U E

NO. 3 (TRAINING) GROUP, ROYAL AIR FORCE.

Resume of Work carried out from

MAY 1918   to   NOVEMBER 1918.

Organisation

       So far as Training was concerned on the formation of the Group, there were four Wings i.e. 7th, 26th, 35th, and 39th; each Wing having some half dozen Training Squadrons.

       After the reorganisation of Units during June and July, the Group consisted of Three Wings i.e. 26th, 35th and 39th; made up of seven Training Depot Stations.

FLYING.

       Throughout the summer the weather was good, and all Stations took full advantage of it, and the Flying Times were exceptionally good. For these months a GRAND TOTAL of 92,852 Hours were flown, this was made up with 61,446 Hours SOLO, and 28,406 Hours DUAL.

       The 26th Wing had the highest number of Flying Hours for any one month -- 6332 Hours for July.

       No. 5 T.D.S. had the highest Monthly Flying Time for any one month -- 2247 Hours for September.

       No. 5 T.D.S. had the highest Weekly Flying Time -- 612 Hours for week ending 23rd September.

       The AVERAGE DUAL PER INSTRUCTOR DAY for the Group was 1-14 Hrs.

       The following comparative table shows the AVERAGE DUAL per INSTRUCTOR DAY by Wings:-

7th Wing	1 hr.	14 mins.
26th Wing	1 hr.	15 mins.
35th Wing	1 hr.	26 mins.
39th Wing	1 hr.	7 mins.

GRAND TOTAL FLYING TIMES FOR MONTHS.

Wing.	May.	June.	July.	Aug.	Sept.	Oct.	Nov.	TOTAL.
7th.	4690-00	3191-12	3454-28	902-30	(Wing disbanded)			12238-10
26th.	4693-10	3796-58	6332-00	5034-50	4000-20	2358-55	1837-40	28511-53
35th.	4695-20	4072-00	5055-50	4684-15	4096-10	2658-45	1678-45	27881-05
39th.	3360-38	3304-41	3761-30	3846-15	3978-35	3548-50	2720-50	24321-19
TOTAL.	17369-08	15154-51	18603-48	15137-50	12083-05	8566-30	6237-15	92852-27

(contd).

(2)

MACHINES.

      During May and the early part of June nearly all instruction was being given to pupils on the D.H.6. and R.E.8., a pupil only getting a very short time on the Service Type of machine. The reason of this was the shortage of this type of machine. However, the situation with regard to these types of machines had materially altered by the end of June, and by the end of July a pupil before proceeding to a Finishing School was putting at least twelve hours on the Service Type of machine. It was not till September that Stations were able to be fitted out with Avros. With this change the Instruction was raised to a much higher standard.

      No. 5 T.D.S. was fitted out with Bristol Fighters, but unfortunately these were not a great success, the engines - Sunbeam Arab - giving a great deal of trouble and spares were practically unobtainable.

INSTRUCTORS.

      On the formation of the Group, there was a deficiency of about sixty Instructors, and Training was severely held up on this account.

      This was at once realised by Squadron Commanders and Wing Examining Officers, and it is through their untiring efforts that by the end of August all Stations were over establishment in Assistant Instructors. However, all Stations felt the lack of Flight Commanders and Instructors with Overseas experience, but this was unavoidable as the supply of those Officers from Overseas was very limited.

      The following comparative table by Wings shows the number of Assistant Instructors turned out:-

Wing.	May.	June.	July.	Aug.	Sept.	Oct.	Nov.	TOTAL.
7th	10	9	7		(Wing disbanded)			26
26th	8	4	6	6	5	6	4	39
35th	7	11	13	13	12	7	4	67
39th	12	1	3	13	4	11	7	51
TOTAL.	37	25	29	32	21	24	15	183

      The following comparative table by Wings shows the number of Instructors sent on Courses to the School of Special Flying.

7th Wing	4
26th Wing	12
35th Wing	18
39th Wing	21

WING EXAMINING OFFICERS.

      The Wing Examining Officers at all Wings have done excellent work, both in raising the Standard of efficiency with regard to Instructors, and the turning out of Instructors. An Instructor was selected at all Stations to become Station Examining Officer, and in consequence the Wing Examining Officer has had more time to devote to General Training Arrangements.

      The times of the Wing Examining Officer of the 35th Wing are excellent.

(contd).

(3)

The following comparative table by Wings shows the DUAL
INSTRUCTION given by Wing Examining Officers:-

Wing.	May.	June.	July.	Aug.	Sept.	Oct.	Nov.	TOTAL.
7th	20-15	7-10	16-15	45-35	(Wing disbanded)			89-15
26th	20-55	43-05	40-00	43-50	46-25	27-45	15-30	246-30
35th	17-05	28-05	52-00	58-30	82-10	27-25	41-30	306-45
39th	12-00	19-35	22-00	9-30	43-55	31-20	17-45	156-05
TOTALS.	70-15	97-55	139-15	157-25	172-30	86-30	74-45	798-35

OUTPUT OF PILOTS.

During the period under review, some 1140 Service
Pilots and 1287 Graduated "A" have been turned out by Stations in the Group.
All Stations were visited by a severe epidemic of Influenza during
September and October.

The change of type of machine from D.H.6 to Avro was
also felt during September, as the personnel were inexperienced in this
type of machine.

The following comparative table by Stations shows the
number of Service Pilots turned out from May 1918 to November 1918 :-

Station.	May.	June.	July.	Aug.	Sept.	Oct.	Nov.	TOTAL.
Easton.	10	45	30	35	22	26	9	177
Wittering.	18	54	30	31	21	24	9	167
Duxford.	14	1	23	22	34	19	13	126
Harborough.	26	32	35	5	2	12	11	123
Fowlmere.	-	10	14	22	20	22	11	99
Thetford.	20	28	19	30-became No. 4 Sch.Nav.&B.D.				97
Feltwell.	12	9	15	9	15	19	13	92
Harling Rd.	17	4	12	9	17	24	7	90
Wyton.	22	19	28	18 became Mobilizing Station.				87
Sedgeford.	23	15	25	19 became No. 3 Fighting Sch.				82
TOTAL	162	197	231	200	131	146	73	1140

GUNNERY.

The chief difficulty that has had to be contended with has
been the selection and obtaining of suitable Aerial Firing Sites.

In many cases Aerial Firing had to be carried out on the
Aerodrome, which was very unsatisfactory. In some cases Sites were
chosen, but owing to agricultural requirements these were unable to be
taken over.

(contd).

(4)

In all, some 1,338,978 Rounds were fired from the air, and the following comparative table by Wings shows the number of Rounds fired for these months:-

Wing.	May.	June.	July.	August.	Sept.	Oct.	Nov.	TOTAL.
7th.	91453	44119	45220	19860	(Wing disbanded)			200652
26th.	83877	42198	56252	69160	44561	32005	52393	380446
35th.	32201	45284	30038	57875	43700	16060	15750	240909
39th.	78402	111643.	71677	81792	59682	53165	60610	516971
TOTAL.	285933.	243244.	203188.	228687.	147943.	101230.	128753.	1,338,978.

At the commencement of the Group, the importance of Camera Gun Work was not fully realised. However, this greatly improved, whereas only 502 Films were exposed in June, in September 3428 Films were exposed.

A great improvement was also noticed with regard to machines carrying out Aerial Fighting Practices. At first, machines were exposing Films at too great a distance, the lack of Instructors with Overseas experience was felt more in this branch of Training than in any other.

The following comparative table shows the number of Camera Gun Films taken by Wings:-

Wing.	May.	June.	July.	August.	Sept.	Oct.	Nov.	TOTAL.
7th.	137	50	151	79	(Wing disbanded)			417
26th.	160	218	281	1192	1019	1360	2040	6270
35th.	30	75	112	909	697	945	1098	3966
39th.	279	160	137	1175	1712	931	1337	5731
TOTAL.	606	503	681	3355	3428	3236	4475	16284.

BOMBING.

The Group has been exceptionally fortunate in having a site for Live Bombing. The Ground at Lakenheath has been turned into an extensive Bombing Ground, this is due to the untiring work of all ranks at the 39th Wing. Some dozen targets have been constructed out of chalk on this ground. A Landing Ground has also been constructed in the vicinity and pupils have been able to land to load up with bombs, and proceed to bomb a given target.

In all, 46½ tons of Live Bombs were dropped at this ground, and the following comparative table shows the number dropped by Wings:-

Wing.	May.	June.	July.	August.	Sept.	Oct.	Nov.	TOTAL.
7th.	330	133	339	308	(Wing disbanded)			1110
26th.	329	24	-	227	308	392	160	1440
35th.	(No Bombing Ground available)				25	59	56	140
39th.	(Bombing Ground not opened.)	100	576	238	987	868	2543	
TOTAL.	659	157	519	1311	565	1438	734	5233.

(5)

It is due to the large amount of Camera Obscura Work carried out at Stations that some very good shooting has been done at this Ground, and the following comparative table shows the number of pupils who have carried out Camera Obscura Tests:-

Wing.	June.	July.	August.	Sept.	Oct.	Nov.	TOTAL.
7th	75	53	22	(Wing disbanded)			150
26th.	37	41	62	71	37	30	278
35th	42	43	63	60	54	18	280
39th	10	23	31	50	74	84	272
TOTALS.	154	170	178	181	165	132	980

The shortage of Bombing Officers has been felt during the whole of this time, the Wing Bombing Officers having to supervise the whole of the Training at Stations.

WIRELESS.
The standard of Wireless has been good, and the system of excusing pupils, who can do 12 words a minute, except for a weekly test has worked very well.   The importance of pupils doing Buzzing with gloves on was not fully realised at first, but latterly this has improved.
The work of the Wireless Officer of the 35th Wing has been very good, especially with regard to the construction of battery positions and stations for   No. 5 T.D.S., Easton-onthe-Hill.

Wireless Telephony is being started at a number of Stations in the Group, and it is hoped that both Instructors and pupils will show great keenness in this branch of Training.

NAVIGATION.
On the formation of the Group there were only three Navigation Officers, and it is through the work of those Officers that suitable Officers have been found and sent on Courses to Winchester. All Stations have now Navigation Officers and great interest has been taken by pupils in this Training.

The shortage of instruments has been felt up to the last month, but now all Stations have complete equipment of Navigation Instruments.

The work of all three Wing Navigation Officers has been exceptionally good, and it is through these Officers that a high standard of instruction has been reached.

(Contd.)

(6)

PHOTOGRAPHY.

The work at many Stations has been interfered with by mist, but a large quantity of very good negatives have been obtained. Special work has been carried out by all sections. Some very good Mosaics for the Air Ministry were turned out by the 35th Wing.

Some difficulty was experienced in the fitting of Cameras for Avros on account of the vibration, but this has been overcome and a standard fitting introduced throughout the Group.

The following comparative table shows the number of printable negatives taken:-

Wing.	May.	June.	July.	August.	Sept.	Oct.	Nov.	TOTAL.
7th.	3195	1155	1507	612	(Wing disbanded)			6469
26th.	-	2151	2551	2444	1104	813	805	9848
35th.	2894	4067	3112	3848	2119	1371	962	18313
39th.	2865	1711	1717	2603	1211	1080	1540	12727
TOTALS.	8954.	9084.	8887.	9507.	4434.	3264.	3247.	47357.

(Signed) A. G. BOARD,   Colonel,
Commanding No. 3 (Training) Group,
Royal Air Force.

Castel Hotel,
CAMBRIDGE,
13th January, 1919.

AGB/DMC.

Select Bibliography

Barker, R., (2002), *The Royal Flying Corps in World War I*, London, Robinson

Bowyer, M.J.F., (1986), *Air Raid! The Enemy Air Offensive Against East Anglia 1939-45*, Wellingborough, Patrick Stephens Limited

Bruton, E., (23/03/15), *Innovating in Combat* at http://blogs.mhs.ox.ac.uk/innovatingincombat/hippisley-hut-hunstanton-wireless-interception-world-war-one/

Castle, I., (2015), *The First Blitz*, Oxford, Osprey Publishing

Clarke, B., (2008), *The Archaeology of Airfields*, Stroud, Tempus Publishing

Clover, C., (2006), *Zeppelins Over The Eastern Counties*, Grantham, Barny Books

Cross & Cockade archive material

Dobinson, C., (2013), *Fields of Deception*, York, Methuen Publishing Ltd.

Faulkner, N. & Durani, N., (2008), I*n Search Of The Zeppelin War*, Stroud, Tempus Publishing

Fegan, T., (2012), *The Baby Killers,* Barnsley, Pen & Sword Military

Francis, P., (1994), *British Military Airfield Architecture*, Stroud, History Press

Franks, N.L.R., (1977), *Jimmy Slater - Fighter Ace*, 64 SQN, Cross & Cockade, Vol. 8, No.2, Summer 1977, 82-85

Grey, C.G., editor, (1969), *Jane's All The World's Aircraft 1919*, Newton Abbot, David & Charles (Publishers) Ltd.

Hart, P., (2008), *Aces Falling*, London, Phoenix

Henshaw, T., (2014), *The Sky Their Battlefield II*, High Barnet, Fetubi Books

Ingleby, H., (1915), *The Zeppelin Raid in West Norfolk*, London, Edward Arnold

Jacklin, D., (2011), *Whin Close Warriors*, Diss, David Jacklin

Lewis, C., (1994), *Sagittarius Rising*, London, Warner Books

Mackersey, I., (2013), *No Empty Chairs*, London, Phoenix

Poolman, K., (1975), *Zeppelins Over England*, London, White Lion Publishers Ltd.

Robinson, D.H., (1973), *Giants In The Sky*, Henley-on-Thames, G.T. Fouls & Co. Ltd.

Simmons, G., (2009), *East Riding Airfields* 1915-1920, Manchester, Crécy Publishing Ltd.

Storey, N.R., (2015), *Zeppelin Blitz*, Stroud, The History Press

Tyler, J.A., (1977), *Norfolk Fledglings: 64 SQN RFC at Sedgeford*, Cross & Cockade, Vol. 8, No.2, Summer 1977, 76-81

Index

Lightning Source UK Ltd.
Milton Keynes UK
UKHW051926131218
333889UK00004B/365/P